ARISTOTLE'S *ETHICS*:
Issues and Interpretations

WADSWORTH STUDIES IN
PHILOSOPHICAL CRITICISM

Alexander Sesonske, General Editor

HUMAN UNDERSTANDING:
Studies in the Philosophy of David Hume

META-*MEDITATIONS*:
Studies in Descartes

PLATO'S *MENO*:
Text and Criticism

PLATO'S *REPUBLIC*:
Interpretation and Criticism

LIMITS OF LIBERTY:
Studies of Mill's *On Liberty*

ARISTOTLE'S *ETHICS*:
Issues and Interpretations

ARISTOTLE'S *ETHICS*:

Issues and Interpretations

edited by
James J. Walsh
COLUMBIA UNIVERSITY
&
Henry L. Shapiro
UNIVERSITY OF CALIFORNIA, RIVERSIDE

Wadsworth Publishing Company, Inc.
BELMONT, CALIFORNIA

WADSWORTH STUDIES IN PHILOSOPHICAL CRITICISM

The idea of a series of Studies in Philosophical Criticism developed in response to a growing problem in American universities. Philosophy can be taught most successfully in small classes; philosophical understanding grows in the course of a dialogue where problems are discussed from diverse points of view by men who differ in experience and temperament. But with the increase in college enrollments, the size of introductory classes has grown larger and the possibility of a dialogue between professor and students more remote. Our hope is that the Studies in Philosophical Criticism will make a dialogue of sorts possible in a class of a hundred, or a thousand, as well as in smaller classes and seminars. Each volume in the series contains a collection of critical writings related to a single classical philosophical text, such as Descartes' *Meditations* or Plato's *Republic*. These critical writings are not substitutes for the classical work, but supplements to it. They should be read in conjunction with the classical text. So used, they will bring to bear on the problems raised by Descartes, Hume, or Plato that diversity of voices and viewpoints which is the heart of the dialogue— and also, we hope, will prompt the student to add his voice to the discussion.

In selecting material for the volumes in the series, the editors have not searched primarily for writings which provide a definitive analysis of the classical text, but have rather selected those papers they thought might be most useful in undergraduate courses in philosophy, both to provoke students into serious engagement with the text and the problems found there, and to present them with a variety of philosophical styles and idioms. Most of the writings reprinted are quite contemporary; they were selected not only for their excellence but also as an indication that many of the classical problems of philosophy persist as centers of current controversy. It is believed that this format also achieves one prime desideratum: it acquaints the student with both the great works of the philosophical tradition and the most contemporary concepts, techniques, and modes of thought.

CONTENTS

INTRODUCTION

There are two ways to read the *Nicomachean Ethics*. We might search in it for a comprehensive moral philosophy—to compare and contrast with those found, say, in Plato's *Republic*, Kant's *Foundations of the Metaphysics of Morals*, or Mill's *Utilitarianism;* we might then epitomize Aristotle's doctrine as naturalistic, teleological, and eudaimonistic. Or we might read the *Nicomachean Ethics* to analyze closely the concepts and arguments employed by Aristotle, searching for an understanding of the several issues he raises, regardless of more comprehensive features. Needless to say, these ways of going at the text do not have to be mutually exclusive, but they often are.

The meaning of the formidable terminology of our epitome (naturalism, teleology, eudaimonism) can be given somewhat as follows. Aristotle is fundamentally a "naturalist" because he treats man as a natural creature—the most highly developed of the animals but still an animal rather than a supernatural soul temporarily sojourning here below. Although Aristotle invites man to become godlike, his appeal is to reason and experience—not to divine commands or sanctions. The rules which the good man obeys stem from his own reason, not from religious revelation or a vision of transcendental ideals; and the satisfactions of the good life are natural elements of the situation, not divinely bestowed rewards. Consequently, man, like the other animals, can act only through the activation of appetites; moral motivation thus cannot be reduced to the struggle of reason as such against appetites as such. Similarly, since pleasure naturally accompanies the successful completion of characteristic animal and human activities, asceticism is ruled out. Aristotle can also be called "naturalistic" in another sense of the term "naturalism": that is, as contrasted with emotivism or prescriptivism as a theory of the meaning of ethical language. While Aristotle does not explicitly discuss such theories, he

1

seems quite clearly to suppose that a main task of ethical language is to convey empirically determinable facts about human nature rather than to express attitudes or prescribe actions alone.

The teleology of the *Ethics* is found in the teaching that man has a function, an end, and that his good is to fulfill it. This function, this end, is the exercise of reason—man's distinguishing feature. However, Aristotle does not imply that natural ends are conscious purposes. Indeed, human purposes are merely one instance of the sequential ordering of means to ends which pervades nature.

The eudaimonism of the *Ethics* is found in Aristotle's statement that *eudaimonia* is the chief good of human life. He carefully distinguishes between *eudaimonia* and pleasure, thus contrasting his position with hedonism, the view that pleasure is the good. *Eudaimonia* is a difficult term, usually translated merely as "happiness." Unlike pleasure, which is confined to limited episodes, *eudaimonia* is an ingredient in a full life; it is identical with or involved in the activity of reason; and it is a rare and demanding condition.

Naturalism, teleology, and eudaimonism—together perhaps with the statement that virtue is a mean between extremes—are the most prominent and characteristic features of Aristotle's moral philosophy. They are the features most readily compared to other moral philosophies, and they may be what the student finds most important. But if he reads the *Nicomachean Ethics* closely, he will find that this epitome, while true enough to much of Books I and X, fails to do justice to most of the work. Much of the *Ethics*, for instance, is taken up by extensive efforts to analyze specific moral virtues. Furthermore, a close reading does not support the assumption that Aristotle intended to offer a comprehensive moral philosophy: How, for instance, is the doctrine of the mean supposed to be related to the philosophical contemplation which is man's natural end and chief good? Ingenious interpretations surmount this problem, but the answer certainly is not obvious; and this is but one such problem. It is only with difficulty, then, that the *Nicomachean Ethics* can be considered as a systematic treatise enunciating a single straightforward doctrine. Henry Sidgwick expresses this reaction by concluding that "on the whole, there is probably no treatise so masterly as Aristotle's *Ethics*, and containing so much close and valid thought, that yet leaves on the reader's mind so strong an impression of dispersive and incomplete work" (*Outlines of the History of Ethics*, reprint of the 1931 edition, London: Macmillan and Co., Limited, 1946, p. 70).

Scholars studying the background to the text can suggest some

e nor to ravish his
from this—it is not a
.ons from those of the
-he can love his own wife
n loves his neighbor's wife—it
.ble, and this does not make them
.hem *other*. What is true of passions is
.e again, the terminology 'excess,' 'the
convenient *imagery*. To neglect one's wife
is deficiency, ner, the mean, to love one's neighbor's wife,
excess. If one were on the quantitative level, it would be more correct
to say, as did the facetious doctor of Frederick II in the remark by St.
Bonaventure, "Not to love any woman is the deficiency, to love them
all is the excess, and the mean is to love one out of every two!" In
reality, we are on the qualitative level: to love one's wife is an action
conforming to the moral rule, to neglect her or to love another man's
wife is an action which does not conform to the moral rule. But to say
that the one is deficiency and the other excess is only a metaphor.
Aristotle uses this metaphor because it is classic; he is not taken in by it.

And that he is not taken in by it Aristotle shows in explicitly
underlining, when the occasion offers, the equivocal nature of the
imagery of the mean. The case of the virtue of magnanimity provides
him with the clearest example. The magnanimous man is worthy of the
highest reward—the honor due to virtue—and he judges himself
worthy of it. That of which the vain man judges himself worthy is
infinitely less. He prides himself, the fool, on paltry rewards. But still,
vanity is an excess and magnanimity is the mean, for the vain man,
however little he judges himself worthy of, still judges himself worthy
of *more* than he deserves, while the magnanimous man judges himself
worthy of that which he *ought* to judge himself worthy, neither more
nor less. Extreme in its nature, the object of magnanimity is no less a
juste milieu because its very grandeur conforms to that 'measure'
which is the moral rule, while the lesser object of vanity is an 'excess'
because it does not conform to it (*E. N.*, IV, 7, 1123b13–14 and
25–26). Aristotle expresses the same thought in looking at the question
from the other end. Even granting the popular assumption that virtue
is a mean when considered in its essence, that is to say, in its *psychological* reality, to love moderately, and neither too much nor too
little—considering it precisely in the order of the good, that is to say,
in its moral reality, it will still be an extreme and a summit. For the
psychologically middling reality in which it is incarnated will, in the

THE HABITUAL STATE
OF IN

If the habitual state which is vir
virtuous things without error, it has above
a kind of kinship between us and virtuous thing   nus making us
spontaneously drawn to them. If the vicious man, who desires entirely
different things, sometimes comes to do virtuous things, it will be
through self-interest, fear, or some other motive foreign to virtue. The
virtuous man, on the contrary, by his very virtue, is made to *want*
virtuous things; when he does them, it will thus be intentionally and
for themselves. (*E. N.*, II, 3, 1105a31–32; cf. V, 9, 1134a2; 10, 1134a20;
1135b25; VI, 13, 1144a13–20). It is in this sense that Aristotle says that
the effect of virtue is to rectify intention (*E. N.*, VI, 13, 1144a20; cf.
E. E., II, 11).

To avoid any misunderstanding, we should begin here by making
two remarks. In the first place, it is important to take note of what
separates the Aristotelian conception of rightness of intention from the
Kantian conception of purity of intention. For Kant, an intention is
pure when the *will* is determined by the maxim which reason enunciates, no account being taken of inclination. Aristotle could not pose
the problem in this way, since he was unaware of the concept of the
will; for him, an intention is right when reason has so pervaded desire
that this latter is drawn toward the very object that reason prescribes.
This pervading of desire by reason is virtue itself, and this is why
virtue rectifies intention.

In the second place, it is necessary to recall that for Aristotle an
'intention' necessarily expresses itself in action, for it is identified with
'decision'. Aristotle has only one word, *prohairesis*, to designate both
the one and the other. A contradiction has often been seen here—does
Aristotle not teach that decision has means for its object, whereas
intention is obviously directed toward an end? (Cf. for instance, W. D.
Ross, *Aristote*, French translation, Paris, 1930, p. 280, Meridian
edition, pp. 195–96; L. Robin, *Aristote*, Paris, 1944, p. 265.) This is to
forget that an Aristotelian 'decision' is only directed to means in order
better to be directed to the end. It is a sufficiently powerful desire for

by deliberation to make us take means to reach the
if it is distinguished from the wish for the end
is not because wish is directed toward the end,
bu   directed toward the end too weakly to take the
mean   successfully. Indeed, it does not even know if those
means   . Thus what Aristotle means to say in making moral
intention a *prohairesis* is that it is an *effective* act; the entirely Platonic
wish or *boulesis* is not yet moral intention for him. Only the desire for
the end which expresses itself in action is moral intention, and this is
why virtue necessarily implies the decisive intention which is *prohairesis* and the exterior act which is *praxis* (*E. N.*, X, 8, 1178a34b1).
The first does not occur without the second.

In what, therefore, does rightness of intention consist? In doing
things which are objectively virtuous *for their own sake* (*E. N.*, II, 3,
1105a32), that is, in proposing as an end in doing these things, not
something other than the things themselves, but the very things which
one does (*E. N.* VI, 13, 1144a13–20). To understand the considerable
significance of this somewhat abstract formula, one has only to glance
at the applications Aristotle makes of it. What is objectively courageous is to stand one's ground in battle and to die in one's place if one
must. But one can stand one's ground because one is ambitious for
civic honors. In that case, one is a good citizen, but not a courageous
man. One can stand one's ground because one has had experience of
danger. One is then a professional, not a courageous man. One can
stand one's ground because of a fiery temperament—animals do as
much, and it is not courage. One can stand one's ground because one
estimates that one will escape from peril; this is optimism, not courage.
And one can stand one's ground because one is unaware of the reality
of the danger, and it is foolishness this time rather than courage (*E. N.*,
III, 11). When, then, is one truly courageous? When one stands one's
ground "for the sake of the beauty of standing one's ground" (*E. N.*,
III, 10, 1115b12–13; 11, 1117a8); or, as Aristotle often says, one is
courageous when one stands his ground "because it is fine" (*E. N.*, III,
11, 1116a11, 15, b3; 1117a17; 12, 1117b9; cf. *E. E.*, III, 1, 1230a32).
Aristotle will return to the same idea in his analysis of liberality (*E. N.*,
IV, 2, 1120a23–24) and of magnificence (*E. N.* IV, 4, 1122b6–7), and
without doubt it is valid for all the virtues in his eyes. Moreover, he
says it explicitly: "The very beauty of its act is the end which virtue
proposes for itself" (*E. N.*, III, 10, 1115b13); "this is a general law
which holds good for all the virtues" (*E. N.*, IV, 4, 1122b7). To do
virtuous things 'for themselves' is thus to do them *for the moral beauty*

which is immanent in them, and conducing to this moral b
constitutes rightness of intention.

In a sense, then, it is accurate to say that for Aristotle it is
objective morality which is primary. First of all there are virtuous
'things', that is, objective ways of acting defined and prescribed by
reason, of which the very rationality makes up the 'beauty', that is, the
value; and it is this objective value which is imparted to our acts by
means of intention. But, and it is here that there reappears in Aristotle's
ethics a kind of primacy of intention, this objective value is *only*
imparted to our acts by intention, that is, only if one takes the
objective value *itself* as the end of one's action. This permits Aristotle
to maintain in a certain way that 'the end justifies the means.' In truth,
the means, which is not desired for *itself,* can have no moral character
in his doctrine. Aristotle can thus teach that it is morally good to
achieve a great and fine action at the cost of a bit of dishonesty (*E. N.,*
III, 1, 1110a19–23). He can teach that truthfulness consists in telling
the truth *for the love of truth* to the exclusion of every other reason,
and that lying consists in saying what is false *for the love of falsehood*
to the exclusion of every other reason—whence it follows that to say
what is false not for the love of falsehood, but for a good reason, is not
a lie (*E. N.,* IV, 13). He can also teach that the act of adultery only
renders the one who commits it adulterous if the act is desired *for its
own sake.* If it is desired under the description of a means to another
end, it is that other end which gives moral character to the act: "If one
man commits an act of adultery to make money and does so, and
another commits it out of lust at the cost of a ruinous amount of
money, the second, in the view of everyone, is intemperate and not
greedy, and the first is a thief and not intemperate" (*E. N.,* V, 3,
1130a24–27). A Greek commentator will conclude quite correctly,
"There is a way of doing bad actions which is not bad. Lying is bad,
but if one lies for a good reason, that is not bad. To sleep with someone
else's wife is bad, but if one does it to overthrow a tyrant, it is not bad.
For badness *only resides in the intention*" (Anonymous, in *Commen-
taria in Ar. Graeca,* vol. XX, p. 142, 9–12). Henceforth one understands that Aristotle insists on the primacy of intention. To be sure, he
has no conception of an intention which is not expressed in action. But
in the end it is intention which makes the value of an act in grasping
the objective value of the thing prescribed by reason (*E. N.,* III, 4,
1111b4–6; 7, 1113b3–6; VIII, 15, 1163a22–23; IX, 1, 1164b1–2).

In thus placing the requirement for rightness of intention at the
heart of his ethics, Aristotle does no more than conform to his

...s of action. If intention ought to be focused on the very act of virtue without subordinating it to anything else, this is ultimately because it is the very nature of moral action to be immanent action which is itself its own end. And so we should of necessity find here the contradiction which Aristotle brought into his *Ethics* by applying his analysis of technical production to moral action. . . : after having shown so decisively that virtuous action is an absolute *end*, Aristotle seems in this analysis to make it a *means* to achieve theoretical contemplation. Ollé-Laprune, among others, has brought out this difficulty and resolved it, insofar as it can be resolved, in discerning, beyond the clumsiness of Aristotle's expression, the profound significance which the relation of virtuous action to contemplation takes on in Aristotle's thought (L. Ollé-Laprune, *Essai sur la morale d'Aristote*, Paris, 1881, Ch. V: "Des difficultés que soulève la morale d'Aristote," especially pp. 154–70). It is his reflections which I wish here to extend a little.

It is noteworthy, first of all, that, whatever the appearances, it could not really be a question for Aristotle of making the act of virtue a *means* properly so-called for achieving contemplation. This is evident if one recalls that for Aristotle, contemplation is an entirely intellectual act—to contemplate is to understand. Now the means to understanding is learning (*E. N.*, II, 1, 1103a15–17). To pay one's debts, to stand firm in battle, are not ways of learning, and they do not make us understand better. And Aristotle knows this as well as anyone (does he not emphasize that the acts which produce a virtue must be the same as those which the virtue produces? *E. N.*, II, 2, 1104a27–b3). Aristotle thus could not have dreamt of establishing a *direct* relation of means to end, of act to act, between the act of virtue and the act of contemplation. And Ollé-Laprune notes correctly that the Christian concept of *merit* is not found in Aristotle. In Christian ethics, merit establishes a relation between the act of virtue and the beatific vision of God, but it is an *indirect* relation: in paying my debts, I merit the vision of God. Paying does not make me see, but it makes me pleasing to God, who grants me the vision. This is an idea foreign to Aristotle. However, for him also there is an *indirect* relation which he establishes between the act of virtue and the act of contemplation. Only the intermediary for him is not God—it is man, that is, the intellect; and it is his intellectualism which allows Aristotle to connect the act of virtue and the act of contemplation. For him, in fact, the same subject is active in both acts, and this subject is the intellect. As an act of intellect, the act of virtue perfects the *intellect*; and as an act of intellect also, the act of

vice degrades the *intellect*. In degrading the intellect, vice ....
contemplation, and in perfecting the intellect, virtue prepares for its
flowering. If we have difficulty conceiving the connection which
Aristotle thus establishes, it is because for us, the subject of virtue and
vice is the *will;* we thus suppose readily that the most vicious man
could be a great philosopher. His will would be perverted, but his
intelligence would be preserved. But for Aristotle the will does not
exist; it is intelligence of which vice is the perversion (vice consists
above all in *thinking* that one ought to do what is wrong, and it is this
error which is the principle of moral transgression. *E. N.*, III, 2,
1110b28–33). The vicious man thus cannot be a philosopher, and
contemplation is the privilege of the virtuous.

Although indirect, the relation of the act of virtue to the act of
contemplation preserves its immanence. What accounts for the value
of the act of virtue is *not* that it can be subordinated (as a means) to
the act of contemplation (only the act of learning is thus ordered); it is
the very fact that it is prescribed by reason. Reason does not prescribe
it because it has reference to contemplation; but it has indirect
reference to contemplation because reason prescribes it and because as
a result, in achieving it I make myself rational. If the philosopher wishes
to pay his debts, this is not because paying his debts will make him
contemplate better; it is because to pay his debts is *rational*, and the
end he proposes in paying his debts is the very rationality of this act of
paying his debts and nothing else. Thus his intention is right and the
immanence of virtuous action is preserved. . . .

PRACTICAL WISDOM: AWARENESS OF DUTY

The word which for Aristotle expresses the concept of 'value' is
the word which we usually translate by "beautiful," *kalos*. This gives
rise to many ambiguities, but they are only ambiguities. Certainly Ollé-
Laprune, for instance, was right to emphasize that Aristotle, as a true
Greek, delights in whatever may be beautiful, even aesthetically so, in
an act of virtue (*Essai sur la morale d'Aristote*, pp. 77–120). But, after
all, one should not forget that, contrary to what is the case for our
word "beautiful," the Greek word *kalos* does not primarily or even
necessarily call to mind the idea of aesthetic beauty. The root from
which it is derived seems to have meant "healthy," "strong," "excellent," "noble;" and in fact, *kalos* often signifies in the actual texts a
thing which is sound, useful, appropriate or fitting for the use one
wishes to make of it; and it is only by extension that it came to

designate aesthetic beauty and moral goodness. (Cf. W. Grundmann, art. 'Kalos,' in G. Kittel, *Theologisches Wörterbuch zum Neuen Testament*, v. III, Stuttgart, 1938, pp. 539–545.) One gathers then that *kalos* can mean "morally good" without connoting any aesthetic idea. That is already the case in Homer, and it is still the case in Aristotle—it is quite unusual for him to use *kalos* to designate aesthetic beauty. Usually the word directly and exclusively calls to his mind moral goodness, which today we call value. And we have seen that for Aristotle, this value consists in the "mean," that is, in the conformity of an action to the rational rule which is its standard and which for us, makes of it a *duty*. . . .

It is only by a paradox carried to an extreme that V. Brochard was able to deny the presence of the idea of duty in the ethics of Aristotle. (V. Brochard, *Etudes de philosophie ancienne et de philosophie moderne*, Paris, 1912, pp. 489–538.) The verb "to owe" ("ought"), *dein*, is in fact one of the words which crop up most often in the *Nicomachean Ethics*. Assuredly, it does not always have a moral sense—but does it always have that sense in English? Setting aside its occurrences in a non-moral sense (approximately 100), Aristotle, in the *Nicomachean Ethics* alone, employs it about 170 times in a sense which is uncontestably moral, as is confirmed by the many times we are told of the closeness and equivalence of duty and the moral good (IV, 2, 1120b4; 1121a1; 3, 1121b4–5; compare also X, 10, 1179b25–26 with X, 1, 1172a22–23). I believe, then, that one cannot fail to recognize that Aristotle placed a distinct idea of moral "duty" (obligation) at the very center of his ethics.

But someone will say that it is still possible that, however central it may be for him, this idea of "duty" (obligation) still remained a confused idea in the mind of Aristotle. (Cf. M. D. Roland-Gosselin, *Aristote*, Paris, 1928, p. 108; L. Ollé-Laprune, *Essai sur la morale d'Aristote*, pp. 81–83.) For in fact, one would search in vain in the *Nicomachean Ethics* for a text where Aristotle has undertaken to define *ex professo* what he understands by "duty" (obligation). But it does not follow that Aristotle did not know very well what he meant by the word; and he has told us enough, although somewhat briefly and only occasionally, for us to be able to see that in fact he had a clear and technically elaborated idea of "duty" (obligation). For, as we have seen, he has expressly identified "what one *ought* to do" with the "mean" of virtue, and this mean itself with "what the right rule commands," which is indirectly to identify "what one ought to do" with "what the right rule commands." And, furthermore, Aristotle

makes this identification directly (III, 10, 1115b12; 13, 1119b17–18). Thus it is not to go beyond the thought of Aristotle to affirm that the very action which is the mean because it conforms to the rule conceived as standard, is *duty* equally because it conforms to the rule—but to the rule conceived this time as *imperative* and as *law*.

Aristotle says expressly that the rule is an imperative and a law: the rule "says," *legei*, but says imperiously (VI, 1, 1138b20); the rule commands, *tattei* (III, 15, 1119b17; VI, 11, 1125b25) or *prostattei* (III, 8, 1114b29); and finally practical wisdom, which is nothing else than the rule, "decrees" (*epitattei*) (VI, 13, 1145a9; cf. 11, 1143a8). Aristotle says perhaps less readily of the rule that it is a law, because that seems to imply the existence of that justice towards oneself whose importance he has been trying to minimize (cf. V, 15, 1138b6–13); but in the end, he says it (cf. IV, 14, 1128a32 and X, 10, 1180a17–22). Certainly it has been doubted whether Aristotle intends to express a true *commandment* by all these words. Thus Ollé-Laprune writes, "This right reason orders, *tattei*, but without in the least playing on words, I shall say that it has for its task much less *to give orders* than *to put in order*. It *orders* man less to do this or that than it *orders man;* *non jubet*, one says in Latin, *sed ordinat*. Even when it *prescribes* an action, *prostattei*, it rather prescribes a beautiful arrangement, a beautiful configuration of the soul and of life, than enunciates an article of law. The *form* which it gives is thus *aesthetic* rather than *legal*. It *arranges* mind and feeling, assigning everything to its place, thus determining conduct; and the analogy is much less to a law which commands than to an internal principle of harmony. *Regulative* without being properly spoken of as *imperative*, it is man himself knowing himself such as he is in the truth of his nature ideally considered." (*Essai sur la morale d'Aristote*, pp. 86–87.) It would be impossible to express with more ability a thought more false. To be sure, this thought is correct in what it affirms: the rule, we have said, is first of all a standard for Aristotle. But it is false in what it denies: as a standard, the rule is nonetheless imperative for Aristotle. Ollé-Laprune has noticed that in order to express its action, Aristotle prefers the words *tattei, prostattei,* the equivalent, according to him, of the Latin *ordinat*, to the word *keleuei*, the equivalent of the Latin *jubet*. But he must admit that the *Eudemian Ethics* employs *keleuei* (*E. E.*, III, 1, 1229a7–11; 5, 1233a22; 1232a36), and now that we recognize its authenticity, that is by no means a negligible piece of evidence. But the great error of Ollé-Laprune is not to have seen that the reason for the preference Aristotle accords to *tattein* and its compounds is precisely

that, from Protagoras on, the technical word to indicate the *imperative* is *epitattein.* . . . As a result, far from merely expressing a formal arranging, the words associated with *tattein* express commands in the strongest sense (cf. for *epitattein, epitaxis,* V, 12, 1136b31; *Politics,* VII, 3, 1325a26; 4, 1326b14; I, 13, 1260b6; for *prostagma,* III, 15, 1119b13; for *prostaxis,* X, 10, 1180a19). They bespeak, not formal causality, but efficient causality (cf. *E. E.,* VIII, 3, 1249a14–15 and *E. N.,* VI, 13, 1145a9); and what finally proves this is that to the act which is expressed by the words *prostattein* or *epitattein,* that which responds in the man who is its object, is obedience (cf. *Topics,* V, 1, 128b19; *E. E.,* II, 1, 1219b30). For the rest, this imperative character, in the strongest sense of the word, which he attributes to the rule is only a part for Aristotle of his general doctrine of the relations of thought and desire. It is obvious for him that thought is the master or that it rules, *archei* (cf. *E. E.,* II, 2, 1219b40; 1220a1; VIII, 3, 1249b10; 21; *E. N.,* III, 15, 1119b7; V, 15, 1138a12, etc.), that it commands, *keleuei* (*De Anima,* III, 10, 433b7), that it is chief, to *hegoumenon* (III, 5, 1113a6), and that desire is subject to it, *archoumenon* (*E. N.,* V, 15, 1138b12; *E. E.,* VIII, 3, 1249b10, etc.), that it obeys, *peitharchei* (*E. N.,* I, 13, 1102b26, 31), and that it ought to be docile, *eupeithes* (III, 15, 1119b12), etc. It is thus beyond doubt that the imperative which the rule is, does not merely arrange or regulate, but it expresses an *obligation* properly so-called. If the rule insofar as it is an imperative makes the act which it commands a duty, it is because it enunciates moral obligation. . . .

Now the right rule is practical wisdom itself (*E. N.,* VI, 13, 1144b27–28). How after this could one refuse to recognize in this practical wisdom which in weighing our actions makes them "beautiful," that is, morally good, and in commanding them, transforms them into "duties," which, in a word, constitutes moral values, what today we call conscience?

PRACTICAL WISDOM: PRINCIPLE OF DECISION

Ollé-Laprune, after also having recognized that it is indeed conscience which Aristotle describes in many passages of the *Nicomachean Ethics,* was astonished that Aristotle did not after this speak of it by name—didn't he have a ready term in the Greek language which he had only to adopt? (*Essai sur la morale d'Aristote,* p. 97). Ollé-Laprune is thinking of the expression *to syneidos,* used by Demosthenes, but better yet, there was at that time in the Greek lan-

guage the word which was later to be used as a technical term to designate moral conscience, *syneidesis,* already used by Democritus (fr. 297).
Why, then, did Aristotle avoid this word? In conformity with his
general interpretation of the ethics of Aristotle, Ollé-Laprune thinks it
is because "Aristotle's idea of responsibility *in foro interno* is, one can
say, *aesthetic* rather than properly *moral.*" (*Essai sur la morale
d'Aristote,* p. 99.) In reality, at the time of Aristotle, the word
syneidesis, if it indeed designates moral conscience, still does not
designate it in all its fullness; it only designates *consequent* conscience
and conscience dealing with *fault,* that by which one judges *after the
event* that one has acted *badly.* Now Aristotle's ethics is an ethics of
virtue, and virtue is infallible for him—what, then, does this ethics
which does not know sin have to do with conscience dealing with sin?
Such a conscience could only exist in the incontinent man, who is the
only one to experience repentance. . . . But Aristotle is hardly interested in the incontinent man. There is thus little room for astonishment
if there is no place in Aristotle's ethics of virtue for *syneidesis,*
conscience dealing with sin. But alongside *syneidesis,* conscience dealing with sin, the Greek language at the time of Aristotle knew *synesis,*
antecedent conscience and conscience dealing with good, which commands us *before* our action to act *well;* and though Aristotle does find
a place for this in his ethics (*E. N.,* VI, ch.11), it is only a secondary
place. What is the reason for this? Still the same: the ethics of Aristotle
is an optimistic ethics which has no place for sin. For an ethics which
acknowledges the possibility of sin, it is important to place in a clear
light not only the role of the consequent conscience which condemns
sin, engenders remorse, and is in the sinner the principle of his reinstatement or his punishment, but still more, the role of antecedent
conscience which, before the act, commands the good and forbids the
bad. Conscience has to have judged for sin to be sin, and its judgment
must be distinguished from free decision for sin to be possible. But the
very end which Aristotle sets up is *to exclude sin,* and this is why the
judgment of antecedent conscience which is *synesis* interests him so
little. What he needs is a judgment upon which action infallibly ensues,
that is, judgment *which is decision itself.* This judgment which is
decision itself is the order issued by practical wisdom, as Aristotle
conceives that. If, then, Aristotle's ethics is not an ethics of conscience
but rather an ethics of practical wisdom, this is not because it is too
"aesthetic," but because it is too "practical," by which I mean, because
it imperiously requires the efficacy of virtuous action, because it
believes so firmly that this ideal of infallibility is the very condition of

true virtue that it is not content with a conscience which leaves the gate open to sin because its judgment is located *before* action. This ethics requires a practical wisdom which excludes the very possibility of sin because its judgment coincides with free decision and thus with action itself.

But the very condition of this infallibility of practical wisdom is the entrance of desire and moral virtue *into its very make-up*—it is because it should result in the efficacy of *virtuous action* that practical wisdom includes desire and virtue. It is for lack of having seen that this and this alone is the justification for that requirement that Walter and his followers were led to misunderstand the entire Aristotelian doctrine of practical wisdom. In fact, when Aristotle tells us that moral virtue "makes the end right" (*E. N.*, VI, 13, 1144a8) or makes intention right (1144a20), that it "makes us achieve the end" (1145a5–6), he does not wish to say that it belongs to moral virtue to "know" the end, or to fix it in some way *without its previously being known,* as if the inclination of virtue were a kind of substitute which here would replace knowledge and make it useless. No—it remains understood that thought is the principle (*Metaphysics*, Lambda, 7, 1072a29–30); thus it belongs to practical wisdom to know the end. Aristotle presupposes that everywhere, and when the occasion offers he says it explicitly (*E. N.*, VI, 10, 1142b32–33). For the rest, let us not forget that what we call ethical "science" or moral "philosophy" is for Aristotle neither "science" nor "philosophy," but practical wisdom, *phronesis*. And Aristotle expressly reserves for the architectonic *phronesis* which is the true "politics"—that is, to ethics—the care of *knowing* the end (*E. N.*, I, 1, 1094a22–b10; VI, 8, 1141b22–25; VI, 12, 1152b1–2). If moral virtue is necessary, it is not at all in order to know the end, it is to *do* it (I, 1, 1095a4–11; cf. VI, 13, 1145a5–6)—in other words, in order *to take effectively for an end* what practical wisdom tells us is an end. For that, in fact, it is not sufficient to know; it is necessary to *desire*, and it is this desire which virtue rectifies. First of all, it keeps the attention of practical wisdom turned toward the true end from which vice displaces it; and, above all, it makes us have the *intention* of attaining this end, an intention which is not a vain wish, but a desire for the end which, after the discovery of the means to it, expands into efficacious decision. And one should not imagine that our explication here goes beyond the thought of Aristotle. Not at all; Aristotle said all that in formal terms—in the *Eudemian Ethics*, it is true, but nothing warrants the assumption that he changed his opinion on this point. In chapter 11 of Book II of the

Eudemian Ethics (1227b12–15), he asks, "Is it virtue which makes intention impeccable, that is, which makes the end right, *in such a way that one makes his decision with the end in view which one ought to adopt*, or, as has been believed, is it the rule?" Those who believed that the moral rule sufficed *to establish action effectively* are Socrates and his followers. Aristotle himself knows that it is efficacious only with the support of desire. It is thus only by confounding the order of specification and the order of effectiveness that one has been able to attribute to Aristotle a species of *moral empiricism* which consists in handing over to virtue and to desire the determination of the end. What Aristotle attributes to them is solely the ability to make one *effectively pursue* the end which practical wisdom has already known and judged as an end.

And it is the same when Aristotle tells us that the role of practical wisdom is to make us *do* the means. Here again it is necessary to see that we are on the level of efficacy. On that level, and if we are concerned with *doing*, practical wisdom is efficacious only in the achievement of the means. Its knowledge of the end is not in fact efficacious; desire must intervene (*Metaphysics*, Theta, 5, 1048a10). On the other hand, its knowledge of the means is efficacious because, at the moment when it knows the means, the desire for the end, which provoked the deliberation, is already in play. In saying that *this*, which is *here and now* doable, is the means for achieving the end currently desired, practical reason includes *this* in the desire presently actual, and practical wisdom *makes* one desire *this* and thus do it. This judgment is efficacious because, by the motive power of desire, it is the imperative of practical wisdom and it is free decision.

This is why we just said that the imperative of practical wisdom *includes* moral obligation. It is certain that this infallible imperative is not the judgment of conscience such as we conceive it, a judgment which can be transgressed against; but if this imperative is not the binding judgment of conscience, this is not because it is *less*—a simple aesthetic ordering—it is rather because it is *more*. It is this judgment, the judgment of *synesis*, and this is why it is the rule which makes the act it commands into a duty; but it is, in addition, swallowed up in this judgment and making it efficacious, desire completely in the grip of virtue—and this is why it is decision.

Thus if Aristotle's ethics is not an ethics of conscience, it is not for lack of having arrived at an elaboration of the idea of conscience and the related ideas of duty and moral obligation; it is on the contrary because it has thought it necessary to push on, to the notion of a

guage the word which was later to be used as a technical term to designate moral conscience, *syneidesis*, already used by Democritus (fr. 297). Why, then, did Aristotle avoid this word? In conformity with his general interpretation of the ethics of Aristotle, Ollé-Laprune thinks it is because "Aristotle's idea of responsibility *in foro interno* is, one can say, *aesthetic* rather than properly *moral*." (*Essai sur la morale d'Aristote*, p. 99.) In reality, at the time of Aristotle, the word *syneidesis*, if it indeed designates moral conscience, still does not designate it in all its fullness; it only designates *consequent* conscience and conscience dealing with *fault*, that by which one judges *after the event* that one has acted *badly*. Now Aristotle's ethics is an ethics of virtue, and virtue is infallible for him—what, then, does this ethics which does not know sin have to do with conscience dealing with sin? Such a conscience could only exist in the incontinent man, who is the only one to experience repentance. . . . But Aristotle is hardly interested in the incontinent man. There is thus little room for astonishment if there is no place in Aristotle's ethics of virtue for *syneidesis*, conscience dealing with sin. But alongside *syneidesis*, conscience dealing with sin, the Greek language at the time of Aristotle knew *synesis*, antecedent conscience and conscience dealing with good, which commands us *before* our action to act *well*; and though Aristotle does find a place for this in his ethics (*E. N.*, VI, ch.11), it is only a secondary place. What is the reason for this? Still the same: the ethics of Aristotle is an optimistic ethics which has no place for sin. For an ethics which acknowledges the possibility of sin, it is important to place in a clear light not only the role of the consequent conscience which condemns sin, engenders remorse, and is in the sinner the principle of his reinstatement or his punishment, but still more, the role of antecedent conscience which, before the act, commands the good and forbids the bad. Conscience has to have judged for sin to be sin, and its judgment must be distinguished from free decision for sin to be possible. But the very end which Aristotle sets up is *to exclude sin*, and this is why the judgment of antecedent conscience which is *synesis* interests him so little. What he needs is a judgment upon which action infallibly ensues, that is, judgment *which is decision itself*. This judgment which is decision itself is the order issued by practical wisdom, as Aristotle conceives that. If, then, Aristotle's ethics is not an ethics of conscience but rather an ethics of practical wisdom, this is not because it is too "aesthetic," but because it is too "practical," by which I mean, because it imperiously requires the efficacy of virtuous action, because it believes so firmly that this ideal of infallibility is the very condition of

true virtue that it is not content with a conscience which leaves the gate open to sin because its judgment is located *before* action. This ethics requires a practical wisdom which excludes the very possibility of sin because its judgment coincides with free decision and thus with action itself.

But the very condition of this infallibility of practical wisdom is the entrance of desire and moral virtue *into its very make-up*—it is because it should result in the efficacy of *virtuous action* that practical wisdom includes desire and virtue. It is for lack of having seen that this and this alone is the justification for that requirement that Walter and his followers were led to misunderstand the entire Aristotelian doctrine of practical wisdom. In fact, when Aristotle tells us that moral virtue "makes the end right" (*E. N.*, VI, 13, 1144a8) or makes intention right (1144a20), that it "makes us achieve the end" (1145a5–6), he does not wish to say that it belongs to moral virtue to "know" the end, or to fix it in some way *without its previously being known*, as if the inclination of virtue were a kind of substitute which here would replace knowledge and make it useless. No—it remains understood that thought is the principle (*Metaphysics*, Lambda, 7, 1072a29–30); thus it belongs to practical wisdom to know the end. Aristotle presupposes that everywhere, and when the occasion offers he says it explicitly (*E. N.*, VI, 10, 1142b32–33). For the rest, let us not forget that what we call ethical "science" or moral "philosophy" is for Aristotle neither "science" nor "philosophy," but practical wisdom, *phronesis*. And Aristotle expressly reserves for the architectonic *phronesis* which is the true "politics"—that is, to ethics—the care of *knowing* the end (*E. N.*, I, 1, 1094a22–b10; VI, 8, 1141b22–25; VI, 12, 1152b1–2). If moral virtue is necessary, it is not at all in order to know the end, it is to *do* it (I, 1, 1095a4–11; cf. VI, 13, 1145a5–6)—in other words, in order *to take effectively for an end* what practical wisdom tells us is an end. For that, in fact, it is not sufficient to know; it is necessary to *desire*, and it is this desire which virtue rectifies. First of all, it keeps the attention of practical wisdom turned toward the true end from which vice displaces it; and, above all, it makes us have the *intention* of attaining this end, an intention which is not a vain wish, but a desire for the end which, after the discovery of the means to it, expands into efficacious decision. And one should not imagine that our explication here goes beyond the thought of Aristotle. Not at all; Aristotle said all that in formal terms—in the *Eudemian Ethics*, it is true, but nothing warrants the assumption that he changed his opinion on this point. In chapter 11 of Book II of the

Eudemian Ethics (1227b12–15), he asks, "Is it virtue which makes intention impeccable, that is, which makes the end right, *in such a way that one makes his decision with the end in view which one ought to adopt,* or, as has been believed, is it the rule?" Those who believed that the moral rule sufficed *to establish action effectively* are Socrates and his followers. Aristotle himself knows that it is efficacious only with the support of desire. It is thus only by confounding the order of specification and the order of effectiveness that one has been able to attribute to Aristotle a species of *moral empiricism* which consists in handing over to virtue and to desire the determination of the end. What Aristotle attributes to them is solely the ability to make one *effectively pursue* the end which practical wisdom has already known and judged as an end.

And it is the same when Aristotle tells us that the role of practical wisdom is to make us *do* the means. Here again it is necessary to see that we are on the level of efficacy. On that level, and if we are concerned with *doing,* practical wisdom is efficacious only in the achievement of the means. Its knowledge of the end is not in fact efficacious; desire must intervene (*Metaphysics,* Theta, 5, 1048a10). On the other hand, its knowledge of the means is efficacious because, at the moment when it knows the means, the desire for the end, which provoked the deliberation, is already in play. In saying that *this,* which is *here and now* doable, is the means for achieving the end currently desired, practical reason includes *this* in the desire presently actual, and practical wisdom *makes* one desire *this* and thus do it. This judgment is efficacious because, by the motive power of desire, it is the imperative of practical wisdom and it is free decision.

This is why we just said that the imperative of practical wisdom *includes* moral obligation. It is certain that this infallible imperative is not the judgment of conscience such as we conceive it, a judgment which can be transgressed against; but if this imperative is not the binding judgment of conscience, this is not because it is *less*—a simple aesthetic ordering—it is rather because it is *more.* It is this judgment, the judgment of *synesis,* and this is why it is the rule which makes the act it commands into a duty; but it is, in addition, swallowed up in this judgment and making it efficacious, desire completely in the grip of virtue—and this is why it is decision.

Thus if Aristotle's ethics is not an ethics of conscience, it is not for lack of having arrived at an elaboration of the idea of conscience and the related ideas of duty and moral obligation; it is on the contrary because it has thought it necessary to push on, to the notion of a

that, from Protagoras on, the technical word to indicate the *imperative* is *epitattein.* . . . As a result, far from merely expressing a formal arranging, the words associated with *tattein* express commands in the strongest sense (cf. for *epitattein, epitaxis,* V, 12, 1136b31; *Politics,* VII, 3, 1325a26; 4, 1326b14; I, 13, 1260b6; for *prostagma,* III, 15, 1119b13; for *prostaxis,* X, 10, 1180a19). They bespeak, not formal causality, but efficient causality (cf. *E. E.,* VIII, 3, 1249a14–15 and *E. N.,* VI, 13, 1145a9); and what finally proves this is that to the act which is expressed by the words *prostattein* or *epitattein,* that which responds in the man who is its object, is obedience (cf. *Topics,* V, 1, 128b19; *E. E.,* II, 1, 1219b30). For the rest, this imperative character, in the strongest sense of the word, which he attributes to the rule is only a part for Aristotle of his general doctrine of the relations of thought and desire. It is obvious for him that thought is the master or that it rules, *archei* (cf. *E. E.,* II, 2, 1219b40; 1220a1; VIII, 3, 1249b10; 21; *E. N.,* III, 15, 1119b7; V, 15, 1138a12, etc.), that it commands, *keleuei* (*De Anima,* III, 10, 433b7), that it is chief, *to hegoumenon* (III, 5, 1113a6), and that desire is subject to it, *archoumenon* (*E. N.,* V, 15, 1138b12; *E. E.,* VIII, 3, 1249b10, etc.), that it obeys, *peitharchei* (*E. N.,* I, 13, 1102b26, 31), and that it ought to be docile, *eupeithes* (III, 15, 1119b12), etc. It is thus beyond doubt that the imperative which the rule is, does not merely arrange or regulate, but it expresses an *obligation* properly so-called. If the rule insofar as it is an imperative makes the act which it commands a duty, it is because it enunciates moral obligation. . . .

Now the right rule is practical wisdom itself (*E. N.,* VI, 13, 1144b27–28). How after this could one refuse to recognize in this practical wisdom which in weighing our actions makes them "beautiful," that is, morally good, and in commanding them, transforms them into "duties," which, in a word, constitutes moral values, what today we call conscience?

PRACTICAL WISDOM: PRINCIPLE OF DECISION

Ollé-Laprune, after also having recognized that it is indeed conscience which Aristotle describes in many passages of the *Nicomachean Ethics,* was astonished that Aristotle did not after this speak of it by name—didn't he have a ready term in the Greek language which he had only to adopt? (*Essai sur la morale d'Aristote,* p. 97). Ollé-Laprune is thinking of the expression *to syneidos,* used by Demosthenes, but better yet, there was at that time in the Greek lan-

practical wisdom which continues from the point at which conscience stops, at the threshold of free decision, and enters into decision and. accompanies action up to its efficacious achievement, which it guides necessarily and infallibly to its conclusion. Antecedent conscience is passed by and is relegated to a secondary level under the name of *synesis,* and consequent conscience, *syneidesis,* disappears because it has no use. Aristotle's ethics is an ethics, not of conscience, but of practical wisdom, by the very feature which makes it a specifically pagan ethics and opposes it radically to Christian ethics: the optimistic humanism which made him believe that sin could be suppressed.

CONCLUSION

One often has the impression that Aristotle himself was aware of what is incomplete and sometimes wavering in his ethics. Certainly, he loves to repeat on every occasion, following Plato, the expressions of modesty with which he introduces his newest and most carefully worked-out positions as though they were mere schematic sketches which could not pretend to exhaust reality, but nowhere does he do this as frequently as in the *Nicomachean Ethics* (I, 1, 1094a25–26; b19–22; II, 1101a27–28; II, 2, 1104a1–2; 7, 1107b14–16; III, 5, 1113a13; 8, 1114b27; 12, 1117b22; V, 1, 1129a11; X, 6, 1176a31; 10, 1179a34). No doubt this insistence is explained in part by the very nature of ethical subject-matter; as changing and elusive as life itself, it is not easily enclosed in rigid frameworks, and one must restrict oneself to more flexible formulae which the circumstances will make precise. The law, Aristotle says neatly, can never be anything but a leaden rule, such as the stone masons of Lesbos use: it must be able to take the shape of the twists and turns of life (*E. N.,* V, 14, 1137b29–32). But if it is true that, in order to enable it to adapt itself to the lessons of experience, Aristotle left the kind of voluntary incompleteness in his ethics which he considers an advantage, he nonetheless recognizes, on occasion, that it suffers as well from another kind of incompleteness which it will be time's role to overcome. And besides, modesty here is only relative: Aristotle knows that he has been a pioneer in this region, and he prides himself on having traced with a masterly hand the outline of every future ethics. But in the end he admits that it is only an outline and that it will be necessary to finish it (*E. N.,* I, 7, 1098a21–26). I wish thus to conclude this exposition of Aristotle's ethics by asking what was missing in this ethics which kept it from fulfilling satisfactorily the aim which inspired it.

Aristotle's ethics purports before all else to be an ethics of the mind, and I have tried to show that it is indeed a rational ethics. The contemplation which it assigns to our life as its end is an activity of pure reason; and if our moral life includes an activity of desire perfected by virtue, this is nonetheless commanded by an activity of reason, the activity of practical wisdom. But, no matter how strongly one insists, as I have, on the primacy of practical wisdom in moral life, and on the rational character which it confers on that life, it must nonetheless be recognized that Aristotle here has only met halfway the demand of the very line along which his thought developed. For him, practical wisdom says that certain conduct is rational and makes that conduct a duty for us—it does not tell us *why* that conduct is rational (*E. N.*, I, 2, 1095b6–7). Aristotle establishes his ethics on the rule which reason enunciates; he refuses to go beyond that and establish this rule itself. It will be the Stoics who go beyond. They are the ones who will discover and elaborate little by little the concept of *natural law*. They will see a law in the very tendencies of our nature because in their eyes it is still reason which expresses itself in those tendencies, God's reason. And they will see that these tendencies are only the inscription in nature of the eternal and divine law, the ultimate foundation of moral obligation. Stoic wisdom, in order to direct life, will thus not be able to content itself any longer with enunciating the immediate rule governing our action: it will have to rest, by way of natural law, on divine law. Thanks to St. Augustine and a whole line of theologians, St. Thomas will be aided by this contribution; and what makes for the originality of his ethics, compared with Aristotle's, is precisely the central position, at the root of moral obligation, which he gives to the knowledge of the first principles of natural law (decked out, through a curious historical accident, with the strange name of "synderesis").

An ethics of the mind, the ethics of Aristotle nonetheless purports to be an ethics of the whole man. In reaction against the pessimism of Plato's first teaching, it intends to give the body its role, and this is the aim of the instrumentist theory (of the relation of soul to body) which is one of its characteristic elements. The body being necessary to the mind of which it is the instrument, the goods of the body and the external goods which are necessary to the flowering of the life of the body, are necessary to the good of the mind, that is, to the virtue and happiness of which they are the instruments. But here again Aristotle's attempt stopped short, and his ethics did not follow the development of his psychology. Aristotle's psychology ended up by making the body not merely an instrument of the mind, which alone is man, but

an integral part of man, who is not man without it. Aristotle's ethics always kept to the Platonic view according to which man is his mind. And it is no doubt this latent Platonism which explains the contradiction, never fully resolved, in which we have indicated one of the major difficulties in the Aristotelian ethics: Aristotle saw very well that moral values could not be reduced to mere means and that they had to be absolute ends: but in order to give them this rank positively, he would have had to see that they were indeed values *of man*, and insofar as man was for him only mind he could not do that. The only fully human value then is necessarily that which alone is the value of pure mind, contemplation; and the properly moral values connected with the body must necessarily be relegated to the instrumental level. Aristotle's attempt to escape this consequence could only end by basing itself on his hylemorphic psychology, and it is for lack of having done this that it remains so full of equivocations.

And finally, as an ethics of the mind, Aristotle's ethics nonetheless aspired to be an ethics for all men. But there it suffers its most brutal defeat. No doubt Aristotle protested against Socratic intellectualism, and he tried to integrate into his ethics values other than the purely intellectual ones which will always be the prerogative of an aristocracy of talent. But, besides pure reason, Aristotle's psychology is aware only of desire; and since this desire is irrational in essence and thus in itself is entirely animal, there can be only one way for it to become a human value, and that is by becoming reasonable in obeying reason. Thus, in the last analysis, reason remains the sole source of value, and Aristotle's attempt to escape from intellectualism falls short. Thus he did not know how to establish true liberty, or to set up an order of values independent of the strictly rational values. He could only have succeeded in that by discovering that the mind itself is not only reason, but also, and above all, will. In that case, after having proclaimed that happiness ought to be accessible to everyone, he would not have had to exclude the bulk of mankind from it. For if the heights of strictly rational contemplation are doubtless always forbidden to the bulk of mankind, the highest adherence to the good is open to the liberty of all men of good will.

REASON, HAPPINESS, AND GOODNESS*

Frederick Siegler

Aristotle says at 1097b22 "To call happiness the highest good is perhaps a little trite, and a clearer account of what it is, is still required." Aristotle thinks that a clearer account can be achieved by "ascertaining the proper function (*ergon*) of man."

There is some dispute as to whether Aristotle is here attempting to give a clearer account of happiness or of the chief good. That he is concerned with happiness is supported by the fact that he had just defined happiness as the final, self-sufficient end of our actions, and that he continues in Ch. 8 with a consideration of popular views of happiness as a check on his own. But Gauthier and Jolif contend that although Aristotle has said that the name of the good is "happiness," he here gives "the essence or the definition not of happiness, but still of the supreme good; these two questions are for him distinct and he treats them quite independently of each other: the fact that the good has for a name 'happiness' does not play a role in the determination of its essence." (p. 54) Consequently they would render the phrase "*potheitai . . . lechthetai*," not as Rackham "we still require a more explicit account of what constitutes happiness," but rather "we still require a more explicit account of what constitutes the chief good." (Ross and Ostwald leave the pronoun "it" without indicating what is the proper referent.) This latter view is supported by the fact that Aristotle does not use the word "happiness" in the course of the argument, and that he concludes "the good of man is the active exercise of his soul's faculties in conformity with excellence or virtue." And he does say that his account is of the Good. But in between these remarks is the suggestion that happiness requires more than a brief time. One hopes that Gauthier and Jolif did not intend to make an issue of this, for it seems a spurious one. It seems perfectly clear that

---

* Printed by permission of the author; to appear in a forthcoming volume of philosophical selections and studies prepared by him and published by Knopf.

the argument about the function of man is meant to reveal truths about
the supreme good and about happiness.

The function of something is discovered, according to Aristotle,
by finding what is both common and unique to that thing.[1] Life is
common to man but not peculiar to him. Nutrition and growth are
shared by plants and animals, and perception is shared by other
animals.[2] Aristotle says that "there remains then an active life (*praktike*) of the rational element."

It is not at all clear in this passage which distinctions Aristotle
intends to suggest concerning reason. It may be, as both Burnet and
Gauthier and Jolif claim that by "*praktike*" Aristotle means to include
contemplation (*theoria*), although Joachim's suggestion to the contrary seems somewhat more sound. Joachim suggests, quite plausibly,
that because Aristotle is concerned here with "the good that is doable"
(*to prakton agathon*), and has set aside the contemplative life for later
consideration (1096a4–5), and because he believes contemplation is not
unique to man, we understand "*praktike*" to include only "a life of
actions" (*praxis*). Again it is not entirely clear how to understand the
distinction between the parts of the rational element, namely, the part
that possesses and conceives reasons (*logon echon*) and the part that
obeys reason (*opipeithes logo*). Joachim suggests that the distinction is
that between originating or formulating reasons or rules and understanding and submitting to reasons or rules formulated by another
mind or faculty. He thinks of the latter notion as applying to a dog or
a child. This interpretation seems faulty because if obeying reason is
part of the rational element, and the rational element is peculiar to
man, then how could that part of the rational element be common to
men and dogs? If there is to be a rational element which is unique to
man, then there must be some distinction maintained between the sense
in which a dog can obey its master and the sense in which a man can
obey reason. If, on the other hand, it is claimed that dogs do have
reason in the sense of being able to obey commands, then the function
of man could not be derived from the notion of obeying commands,
since it would not be unique to man. Gauthier and Jolif merely
postpone this issue by agreeing with Grant, Rassow, Susemihl and
Burnet that this sentence is a gloss taken from Bk. 1, Ch. 13. The
distinction between the "two senses" seems somewhat less difficult to
understand. Aristotle intends to distinguish between having the ability
to reason and the activity of reasoning. A man who is sleeping may
have the ability to reason but he is not reasoning.[3] If, then, the first
distinction is between originating reasons for acting and acting on

reasons given by others, both of which activities are peculiar to humans, since they are parts of the rational element which is said to be peculiar to man; and if the second distinction is between acting on reasons (self or other conceived) and simply having reasons for acting (self or other conceived); then, how is it that "the activity . . ." has a greater claim to be the function of man? (1098a6) For if we grant that all of these are elements peculiar to man since they are either parts of "the rational element" or senses of "life of the rational element," then all have equal right to be called the function of man. Perhaps there is an implied argument that the function of man is to be specified in terms of his *doing* something. And since having reasons for acting is not itself doing something, and acting in accordance with reasons is doing something, then this gives "activity" the greater claim. But this is less an argument than a clarification of the enterprise, for Aristotle is examining "the *active* life of the rational element" (my emphasis), and consequently it should be clear that actually *acting* in accordance with reasons is the sense of the term "active life" (*praktike*), and simply having reasons or the ability to reason in action is not. Consequently *"kurioteron gar aute dokei legesthai"* should be rendered not as in Ostwald, "For activity, it seems, has a greater claim to be the function of man," but as Ross and Rackham, "Since this seems to be the more proper sense of the term." Finally, it is not clear how to understand the distinction between "activity of the soul in conformity with a rational principle" and "not without it (a rational principle)." Stewart and others have claimed that the distinction is that between contemplation and obedience to reason by the appetites (moral virtue), but Gauthier and Jolif's suggestion that Aristotle is not here concerned with contemplation but solely with moral virtue seems more plausible. Their positive suggestion about the passage is that we understand Aristotle to mean that "it is not necessary, for an act to be morally virtuous, that it explicitly and consciously refer to a rule, (but) it is sufficient that the reference be implicit and it could be unconscious." But this suggestion should be clarified. There is more than one distinction which Aristotle might have in mind here. He might be referring to the previous distinction between acting on a reason or rule of one's own formulation and following somebody else's rule or reason. He might mean to suggest the distinction between acting for the sake of a rule and acting in a way which conforms to or exhibits a rule. Or he might be suggesting a distinction between deliberately following a rule and following a rule through habit. For example, I brush my teeth not after deliberation of the pros and cons, but automatically; however, not automatically as a

machine. I could report why I do it but my report would not be on my daily deliberations before doing it.

Aside from these difficulties in understanding this passage there are difficulties in specifying exactly how humans differ from other animals. How is one to characterize the behaviour of a watch-dog or even of a cat stalking a bird? Do they act in accordance with reasons? Of course there are reasons for what they do, but do they have reasons for what they do? Can they be said to act for the sake of reasons or rules? I have been puzzled for some years about how to describe a poodle that I know who when he sees young kittens scratching the furniture in his master's home, barks at them and knocks them away with his nose or paw if they disregard his bark. Is the dog giving commands, issuing orders or rules? But leaving aside, for now, this difficulty about how to specify in detail the peculiar ability of humans to reason in their actions, it seems plausible to say that there are ways in which human beings alone can be said to act on or for the sake of reasons. In what follows I shall not suppose that we have clearly specified the line between peculiarly human behaviour and other animal behaviour; rather I shall, when necessary, specify action-descriptions which seem indisputably to be peculiar to human beings. For the most part I shall be concerned with (1) three senses of a "function" and (2) two senses of "reasoning" both of which are applicable to human beings alone.

Now, what does it mean to say that acting for the sake of reasons is the function or proper function of man?[4]

Consider the argument in the following form:

1. Man has a function.
2. The function of man is determined by what is peculiar to man.
3. What is peculiar to man is acting on reasons.
4. The function of man is acting on reasons.

Suppose for the moment that we understood what was meant by "the function of man." Then there would still be some problem as to how Aristotle establishes that man *has* one. He suggests two considerations or arguments. (1) Since the carpenter and shoemaker have their own functions and spheres of action, presumably man as man has one too (by nature). (2) Since each part of the body "has its own proper function, so man too has some function over and above the functions of his parts."

Now these arguments look inconclusive. For it is not clear what

sort of implausibility or absurdity would be reached by asserting that carpenters have functions but man as man does not. Or that although the parts of man have functions man as a whole does not. If Aristotle were to assert as a general truth that every natural thing has a function then of course it would follow that man has one. But he does not assert this. And if he did there would be difficulties about e.g. the functions of the appendix. And presumably we should require some argument to support such a view. But even if, for the sake of continuing, we accept that man *has* a function, what does this *mean?*

Now we do speak of the flute player as having a function in an orchestra, but it is not clear what could be meant by the function of the flute player *qua* flute player. According to Aristotle the function of the flute player is to play the flute. Function, here, means "what constitutes being a flute player." It is of some importance to note that if a flute player plays the flute he does not thereby discharge any moral or other kind of obligation, and he does not thereby benefit from playing the flute.

If by function of man Aristotle means what he means when he speaks of the function of a flute player, and by function of a flute player we understand "doing what constitutes being a flute player," then Aristotle means by function of man "doing what constitutes being a man." Now just as playing the flute is peculiar to being a flute player, so acting on reasons is peculiar to being a man. Consequently when Aristotle says that the function of man is acting on reasons he must or can only mean that men alone act on reasons, or that acting on reasons is what constitutes being a man. And again, by parity of reasoning, when a man acts on reasons he does not thereby discharge any moral or any other kind of obligation, nor does he thereby necessarily benefit from acting on reasons.

We have considered one sense of function which Aristotle might be said to have in mind when he says "The (proper) function of man is an activity of the soul in conjunction with the rational element." The sense we have discussed might be called a descriptive sense of "function." In this sense we speak of the function of some object as that which the object characteristically does, or is designed to do. For example the function of the blackjack is to stun temporarily. That is its function, purpose, or role in life. From this truth about the function of the blackjack it does not follow that anyone ought morally to use that tool; and if anything practical follows, it is that if you want to stun somebody then you ought (not morally) to use a blackjack.

There is another sense of function which is not so aseptic as this.

Suppose somebody said "Johnson is ruining the country: after all the function of government is to leave all commercial affairs to private enterprise. He is going beyond the proper function of government." The critic is not describing how in fact the government is run or what in fact constitutes the workings of a government. Rather he is criticizing the activities of our government in terms of what he thinks ought to be the sphere of governmental activities. This notion of function might be spoken of as "the evaluative or ought sense of function."

These two notions of function can be exemplified by comparing discussion by scholars of the function of the medieval university, with discussion by contemporary educators of the function of today's university. The latter group speak in the idiom of what ought to be, recommendation, and advice. The former group speak in neutral terms. The former group are trying to say things which are true, e.g., "the medieval university functioned as a proving ground for clerics." The latter group are trying to say things which ought to be true, e.g., "the function of the university is to train young minds for the professions." Their point might be put by reference to something which may *be* true of universities, e.g., "although today's university *functions* as a mating ground for overgrown adolescents, its *real* or *proper* function is to train young minds for the professions."

We now have two notions of function. The first describes what something characteristically *does* do, and the second states what something *ought* to do. It seems possible that a third notion of function could be developed. There is general agreement that Aristotle's discussion of function is in some way derived from that in Plato's *Republic* 352dff, where examples of tools, horse, and sense organs are developed. One example of the notion of a function is Plato's analysis of the *orgon*, the work or function of an instrument or tool such as a knife. The function is determined by the producer's purpose in making it or the user's purpose in using it. Joachim comments: "the purpose is not sheerly external: i.e., the work of the tool and the tool's own nature (its material, shape, etc.) are necessarily adjusted to one another. The work of cutting demands, for example, steel (not wood), and steel of a certain shape. To that extent the tool, in serving the purpose of the craftsman, is fulfilling itself, its own destiny. A knife which will not cut is not merely a bad knife—it is not a knife at all, but for example, a mere piece of steel: steel of a certain shape (what we call a 'knife') is only itself in cutting." Joachim cites Plato's illustrations of the horse's function to make a similar point. He admits that in fulfilling **its** function "to bear its rider safely and quickly" the horse is fulfilling a

purpose "imposed on it by man. But obviously man, in using the horse for his purposes, is taking advantage of the natural powers of the horse: i.e., the horse, in doing the work which man sets it, is also realizing its own nature or *phusis*, exercising a function in which it expresses its self. In other words the horse, in making its contribution to the well-being of man, is also achieving its own well-being." The horse thereby "fulfills its own natural tendencies and powers, as well as certain wants of man." (p. 48)

From this we might develop what could be called the beneficial notion of function. Man, in doing what is peculiar to him or what his natural powers enable him to do, is thereby realizing his own nature and therefore achieving his own well-being or benefitting himself.

We now have three notions of a function: (1) descriptive, what an x characteristically does, (2) evaluative, what an x ought to do, (3) beneficial, what an x does that benefits him or leads to his well-being.

We have considered the argument in terms of function in the first sense, and now we shall consider it in the third, and then the second senses. Using the third sense of function the argument would run:

1. Man has a function (doing what is beneficial to man).
2. What is beneficial to man is doing what is peculiar to him.
3. What is peculiar to man is acting on reasons.
4. What is beneficial to man is acting on reasons.

Now this conclusion 4 follows from 2 and 3, but there is some unclarity as to how to go about determining the meaning and truth of 2. In fact it is 4 that is attractive in this argument, and it does have an air of truth about it. For surely, if a man has goals or aims in life it is unlikely that he will achieve his aims if he does not act on reasons. In fact, if a man has aims then it seems that if he does not act on reasons to achieve his aims, in a clear sense he cannot be said to have *achieved* his aims. A man whose aim it is to win a chess match is less than half glad to win by forfeit. He does not thereby achieve his aim, rather it comes to him. In another way this conclusion seems plausible. We as human beings do seem to place value on rational activity, activity which involves reasoning. And if a person were to spend his life eating and sleeping we might pity him and encourage him to do something (which involves reasoning). For we think it to a man's benefit to engage in reasoning. But though in some ways the conclusion seems quite plausible, its plausibility does not derive from the premises since

2, a crucial premise, is by no means clear, or if in a way understandable, it is not clearly true.

Another difficulty in this third notion of function is that *if* it does indeed derive from Plato's discussion of the function of a knife, horse, or eye, etc. it is not clear how this aids in understanding what Aristotle might have in mind in speaking of the function of man. Now it is certainly true, in Plato's examples, that there is some notion of benefit or well-being involved in a thing's performing its function, but it is the user who is benefited when, for example, the knife performs its function, and it is difficult to attach any clear sense to the talk of the knife's "fulfilling itself, its own destiny."[5] Let us ask this: Does the notion of the knife's fulfilling a function have any bearing on *its* happiness or moral goodness? Obviously not. There is no notion of the happiness or moral goodness of a knife, and it is difficult to see how the knife could be said to benefit in any way. But this is exactly what Aristotle has to say if an analogy between the function of a knife and the function of a man is to have any relevance to the discussion of the happiness or goodness of man.

Now consider the case of the horse. Does the notion of the horse's function have any bearing on its happiness or moral goodness? Clearly not the latter. There is some suggestion by Joachim that if a horse fulfills its function it is doing something that benefits it, but it seems that such a suggestion is gratuitous. To say that a work-horse is "realizing its own nature or *phusis*, exercising a function in which it expresses its self . . . achieving its own well being, etc." suggests that a horse is happy in doing what man wants it to do, and there seems to be no good reason to believe such a thing. There is no indication as to how one is to establish such a claim. That a horse is kept under lock and key even after it has been trained to contribute toward "achieving its own well-being" suggests, if anything, the contrary.

If what I have argued is correct, then the notion of the function of the knife, horse, or eye cannot really give us a beneficial notion of function that could be used to elucidate the happiness or moral goodness of man.

Difficulties also arise from employing sense 2 of function.

1. Man has a function (doing what man ought to do).
2. What man ought to do is what is peculiar to him.
3. What is peculiar to man is acting on reasons.
4. What man ought to do is act on reasons.

For one thing, if "ought" is taken as a moral ought, then it is not clear that 2 is true, or how we should settle the issue of its truth. And even if this were true and it were a moral ought, 4, which would follow from 2 and 3, does not seem acceptable as it stands.

For although it might well be beneficial to man to act on reasons, it does not seem right to say that if a man acts on reasons he is thereby acting as he ought. And this is because a man can act on reasons and still be morally wicked. Of course it is true that the notion of acting on reasons or for the sake of reasons is sometimes construed as acting on right reason, where this comes to "acting on reasons for morally good goals." After all when we say that a man is reasonable we mean more than that he acts on reasons; rather we mean that his reasons are good ones, and his *aims* are good ones. And in that sense of acting reasonably, the conclusion 4 seems quite plausible, though perhaps a bit circular and thereby trivial, namely, what man ought to do is to act reasonably, i.e., to act on good reasons for good aims. But if the conclusion is taken in this sense then so must the premises be taken in this sense. And then in premise 3 "acting on reasons" must mean "acting on reasons for good ends." But in that case premise 3 is *false*. For what is peculiar to human beings, we agreed, is acting on reasons, or for the sake of reasons, but not in the sense of having the right reasons, or the right ends in view. Although it does seem to be peculiarly human to help a lady because she is in need, an action for the sake of a reason, it is, unfortunately, no less peculiarly human to shoot a lady because she is a bore, an action for the sake of a reason. Acting for the sake of reasons is perhaps peculiar to human beings, but it is no more or less peculiar to human beings to act with the right reasons or for the right ends than it is to act for unjustifiable reasons or for the wrong ends.

Consequently, if we understand "acting on reasons" in premise 3 to refer to what is common to Hitler and Churchill, namely acting for the sake of reasons, then premise 2 would be false, and the conclusion 4 would not be established by the argument. On the other hand, if we construe "acting on reasons" to mean "having the right reasons for the right ends" then even if we accept premise 2, premise 3 would be false, and the conclusion, though it seems trivially true, would not be supported by the argument. It may be that Aristotle is suggesting that if a man wants to achieve his aims, and if he wants to be morally virtuous, then a *necessary* but not sufficient condition is acting for the sake of reasons, or on reasons. If one does not reason in his activities he will not be able to achieve his aims, including happiness, nor will he be

able to become morally good since moral goodness involves at least reasoning with regard to one's activities.

Aristotle now offers an analogy between the function of man and the function of a harpist. Is Aristotle hoping to explicate further the concept of happiness or the concept of good? Is he hoping to show some connection between being happy and being good?

It seems unquestionable that the function of a harpist is to play the harp, if by function we mean what he *qua* harpist characteristically does. Furthermore it seems unquestionable that the function of a good harpist[6] is to play the harp well. Now, by parity of reasoning since the function of man is acting on reasons (that is what is peculiarly characteristic of man *qua* man) a good man would be a man who reasons well or is a good reasoner.

But here again "reason well" is equivocal. It could mean (1) that he has reasons which *justify* his actions, or (2) that his reasons are well or efficiently designed for his purposes, whatever his purposes may be. Reasoning well, therefore might imply that the agent is (1) morally praiseworthy, or (2) praiseworthy in calculation or efficiency. Now I think that 1 in practice requires 2 since one can hardly do the morally right thing if he is poor in calculation. This point is discussed by Aristotle in Bk. 6 Ch. 5–13 where he finally concludes that the morally good man must have practical wisdom which is concerned with the calculation of means for reaching one's ends. But it is clear that 2 in no way requires 1, for the man who is clever in deliberation or calculation concerning his aims does not necessarily have morally praiseworthy aims. Such a man Aristotle says (1144a24ff) has cleverness, and if he has noble aims then his cleverness deserves praise, but if the goal is a bad one then the cleverness is knavery or smartness.

Now suppose that Aristotle has in mind the first sense of "reasons well." In that case there is no parallel with the harpist; for the harpist and the good harpist are related solely in terms of performing that which is his peculiar function or ability, namely playing the harp. But we agree that the peculiar function or ability of a man is acting on reasons in a neutral sense; that is, excluding the issue of the moral or beneficial nature of the ends, for it is no more or less unique for a man to make plans for a new hospital than it is for him to make plans for a bank robbery. Now if this is so, then it just does not follow that a man who performs his peculiar function well is doing something morally praiseworthy. All that follows is that if a man performs his peculiar function well his reasons reveal careful design and deliberation and efficient planning. And consequently if Aristotle has in mind sense 1 of

"reasons well" then the analogy between the harpist and man is gone. Consider the argument as follows:

1. The function of a harpist is to play the harp.
2. A good harpist plays the harp well.
3. So in general if the function of an X is to f, then a good X must f well.
4. The function of man is to act on reasons or reason in his actions.
5. A good man acts well on reasons or reasons well in his actions.

Now grant for the present purposes the truth of 3 as established by or supported by premises 1 and 2. Premise 4 is true if function means what it does in premise 1, namely, that which constitutes being a man, what is peculiar to being a man. But then 5, the conclusion, does not follow if by "reasons well" Aristotle means "has reasons which justify his actions," for (a) "good" in premise 3 is neither a moral nor a beneficial good, (b) "reasons" in premise 4 is morally and beneficially neutral, and (c) since "good" and "reasons well" in the conclusion, if it is to follow logically from the premises, must retain the same sense it has in the premises. Consequently, there is no room for sense 1 of "reasons well" in this argument.

Now on the other hand, suppose Aristotle has in mind the second sense of "reasons well." In that case the parallel with the harpist is maintained. For since it is the peculiar function or ability of man to act on reasons, it would follow that a man who was skilled at or had a high standard in that particular function is a man highly skilled in reasoning; he is a man who deliberates carefully, plans with precision, and organizes his activities so that he can achieve his aims, whatever they may be. But of course, from this it does not at all follow that a man who performs in accordance with the function of man (reasoning) is *eo ipso* a morally praiseworthy man. Nor does it follow that a man who performs his function (reasoning) skilfully is *eo ipso* a morally praiseworthy man. Acting on reasons or having reasons for one's actions may be a necessary condition for moral worth, and being a *skilful* reasoner may be a necessary condition for moral worth. But neither of these conditions is sufficient for moral worth, since a clever bank robber has reasons carefully designed for his aims. It is true, as Aristotle says, that "any action is well performed when it is performed in accordance with the appropriate excellence," but since the peculiar ability or function of man is acting on reasons, and the excellent functioning of man is having well designed reasons, it does not follow that an action that is well performed is a morally praiseworthy action.

Reason, Happiness, and Goodness

Now if Aristotle thinks that a man will be happy if he p
actions in accordance with carefully designed reasons, then it ...
that such a man whether he has good aims or bad aims, will be happy.
And this may or may not be true. But if it is true then it by no means
follows that happiness is activity of the soul in accordance with *virtue*,
if by "virtue" Aristotle means having morally praiseworthy aims. Only
if Aristotle means by "virtue" the exercise of the peculiar ability to
deliberate and reason about aims might it be true to say that happiness
is activity of the soul in accordance with virtue. But then this is only
to say that a man with moral or immoral aims is happy if he reasons
well about his aims. And so if this argument about the function of man
is meant to elucidate the concept of happiness, then Aristotle is
justified in concluding only that a man is happy if and only if he
reasons well about his aims. But Aristotle wants the conclusion that
happiness is virtuous activity of the soul (1099b25), and he wants
virtue to mean having virtuous or praiseworthy aims, good and noble
ends.

Furthermore, if Aristotle thinks that human good, or what is
morally praiseworthy in human action, is activity in accordance with
the efficient functioning of man, then it follows from his argument
that an action is morally praiseworthy if and only if it is performed in
accordance with the efficient functioning of the peculiar ability of
reasoning. But that conclusion does not seem to be correct. For as we
have suggested, a man might reason well about evil aims, thereby using
well his peculiar ability and not be morally praiseworthy. To act on
well designed reasons may be a necessary condition but it is certainly
not a sufficient condition for moral praise. So the only conclusion
justified by his argument is that if a man reasons carefully and
successfully he is morally praiseworthy. And that conclusion is quite
false. Of course Aristotle does not want to come to that conclusion.
He wants to conclude that the function of a good man is the good and
noble or right and proper performance of rationally based actions. And
although this conclusion seems quite plausible it does not follow from
his argument. And this is simply because the argument about the
function of man refers to what Aristotle considers to be peculiar to
human beings; yet this peculiarity does not single out morally praiseworthy aims from morally blameworthy aims. It singles out the ability
to act on or for the sake of reasons. And because he referred to the
ability to act on or for the sake of reasons, his claim about the peculiar
ability of man seemed to be true. But if he had claimed that the
peculiar ability of man was to act on reasons for morally praiseworthy

aims, his claim about the peculiar ability of man would be false, since it would imply that the ability to act on reasons for morally blame-worthy ends is not equally peculiar to man. And because the claim about the peculiar function of man did not separate morally praise-worthy aims from morally blameworthy aims, it is no wonder that Aristotle cannot come to any conclusions about what constitutes morally praiseworthy actions if such conclusions are based solely on the peculiar function of man.

We may have been tempted, as perhaps Aristotle was tempted, by a misleading parallel between the harpist and man. A harpist *qua* harpist is praised for performing his function well. There is nothing morally praiseworthy about that. But man *qua* man can be praised on two separate (though perhaps related) accounts. He can be praised for performing his function well. That is by no means moral praise. And he can be praised for performing his function well for morally praiseworthy ends or aims. And as I have suggested, it may be a necessary condition for moral praise that a man be able to reason well about his aims, but that is not sufficient. He must have the right aims. And having the right aims is unfortunately not any more peculiar to human beings than having the wrong aims. But to be a moral man one must be more than an efficient reasoner. There may be some sense in saying of an efficient reasoner who has aims we believe to be wrong that he is not *really* reasoning, but (1) that sounds as though one is trying to defend a thesis at any cost, and (2) surely what such a man is doing is peculiar to man.

Now a few summary and concluding remarks. It seems true to say that human beings alone have the ability to act on reasons, to plan to achieve their aims, and to reason about what their aims will be. Whether or not it is because of this fact, it seems true also that human beings desire to act on reasons, to reason about their activities in order to achieve their aims, whatever their aims may be. And further it seems true that reasoning about one's activities is a necessary condition for achieving one's aims. Again, it seems true that behaviour which is open to moral criticism involves acting on reasons. Again, it seems plausible to say that we conceive happiness to be the achievement of our aims, whatever they may be. Although this last claim is perhaps not un-objectionable, even if we take it to be true and accept its implication that a man who has evil aims which are satisfied by careful reasoning can be happy, it would not follow that we should bestow moral praise on a man who is happy through the achievement of aims which we deplore. We might *wish* that he were not so happy, but *pace* Plato and

Norman Vincent Peale (for very different reasons), unfor
that does not make the unjust man unhappy.

Finally, we can say that a man who does act on reasons for ends
we consider to be noble and good may be happy as well, if, that is, he
is not, as Aristotle says, on the rack. This man we should morally
praise; we should call him happy and virtuous. Consequently, if we
know what is a right aim and what is a wrong aim, and we act
efficiently in accordance with reason we shall be both happy and
virtuous. That Aristotle has not shown, at least in the argument we
have considered, that the unjust man is necessarily unhappy, is not so
surprising, for Aristotle did say that he presupposed that his readers
already wanted to become good. This leaves those who do want to
become good with the question "How do we discover what are the
right aims?" Is it by contemplation? Is it by watching the good man,
i.e., the man with right aims? If the latter, then how do we pick out
the good man? That may be no less difficult than picking what are the
right aims.

I have argued that Aristotle does not prove his point at 1097b23ff.
But I am inclined to think that two arguments deriving in great part
from other sections of the *Nicomachean Ethics* can be presented in
favor of the view that only the virtuous man can be happy. Furthermore, it can be argued that because a reasonable man can come to
understand such an argument it follows that a reasonable man will seek
to become virtuous at least in part because he desires to be happy. And
this is in conformity with Aristotle's own view, namely, "all virtues we
choose partly for themselves . . . but we also choose them partly for
the sake of happiness, because we assume that it is through them that
we will be happy." (1097b2–5)

The first consideration is Aristotle's claim that virtue is by nature
pleasant. (1099a6–21) Now Aristotle says many things about pleasure
in the *Nicomachean Ethics* some of which have the appearance at least
of being incompatible; and, further, "pleasure" does not seem to be the
right word (though it seems to be the right translation of "*hadus*").
What Aristotle might have in mind is something like this: a virtuous
man in doing what he knows to be right is doing what he wants to do.
He wants to do it because it is right and not primarily for another
reason or some ulterior reason. The wicked man does what he knows
to be wrong but he is not thereby doing what he wants to do. And
furthermore he does what he knows to be wrong not because it is
wrong but because of some object he hopes to attain. The reason why
"he is not thereby doing what he wants to do" is that under some

specifications of a wicked act he may not want to do it or wish that he
had not done it. For example, if a man tries to rob a bank and fails (due
to no incompetence, but let us say, due to fortune, e.g., there happened
to be an off-duty policeman passing by) he has done a wicked act—
attempted to rob a bank—and because he did not get what he wanted,
namely, the money, he is likely to wish that he had not done what he
did. He does not want to do a wicked act under the specification
"attempted robbery." On the other hand if the virtuous man fails (due
to no incompetence) to succeed in, for example, catching a thief or
saving a drowning child, he does not wish that he had not attempted.
On the contrary he has done what he is glad that he has done, namely,
his best to catch a thief or to save a drowning child. He does not wish
that he had not made an attempt, for the attempt is itself virtuous (just
as the attempt to rob is in itself wicked) and his aim is to do what is
virtuous under any specification. The wicked man aims to do what is
wicked only under specifications of a certain kind of success. For this
reason we might think of "pleasure" as contingently connected with
wickedness since it comes only with a specific form of success. And
similarly we might think of "pleasure" as necessarily (or by nature)
connected with virtue since it comes with any virtuous act.

Aristotle's notion of happiness involves activity in which one
wants to engage. Activities which are engaged in for their own sakes
are thought of as superior in that *inter alia* they are less dependent on
good fortune. Such activity is less vulnerable to impediment, and again
Aristotle thinks of unimpeded activity as being "pleasurable" or "en-
joyable." (1172a19–1177b11) But even those activities which we do
for their own sakes are impeded by circumstances in a way that
virtuous activities are not. A man may walk for pleasure but hurt his
leg and no longer get pleasure from walking. But a man who does what
he believes to be right is not similarly limited. For while doing one's
best to walk may be painful and regretted by a man who normally
walks for pleasure, doing one's best to save a drowning child is not
similarly painful or regretted. That he did his best is what he wants to
have done.

The second consideration is Aristotle's claim that while there are
three forms of friendship the highest form "is that between good men
who are alike in excellence or virtue." (1156b6) Aristotle discusses the
two lower forms of friendship as reciprocal relations which last as long
as both parties can perform their tasks. It seems clear that although a
wicked man can partake of these forms, for utility or for affection,
there are occasions when although a man is unable to perform his tasks

he needs help or attention. Further, if the wicked man is found out he might not be trusted even in a reciprocal friendship. Even if we think of friendship among scoundrels, we are inclined to think of mutual distrust, and betrayal, and, of course, there is always the possibility that one man will reform and give up the arrangement with a scoundrel.

But aside from the reciprocal friendships engaged in for utility or affection Aristotle speaks of the highest form which involves loving someone for what he is and not for what he can do for you. It might be argued that men do want to partake in such a form of friendship, both because they admire others for what they are and because they want to be admired for what they themselves are. If a desire to participate in such a form of friendship is a necessary or important condition for happiness then surely the wicked man cannot be happy since he cannot be admired for what he is and he knows it. For since he knows that he does what is wrong he thereby knows that those (if there are any) who claim to love him for what he is are either liars or fools.

Two final points. The two considerations sketched above depend heavily on the notion of doing something or desiring something for its own sake as apposed to doing something for a further purpose or end. Indeed, it might be suggested that most of the force of these two considerations is independent of the issues of virtue and wickedness. For suppose a man does what he believes to be wicked and does it for its own sake. In accordance with the first consideration such a man would not wish that he had not made an attempt (unsuccessful through no incompetence) since his aim is to do what is wicked under any specification. In accordance with the second consideration such a man might participate in the highest form of friendship in so far as he can be admired for what he is by people with similar aims or purposes.

Second, both Plato and Aristotle assume, as I did in my sketch, that the wicked man knows that he is wicked at least in the sense of being in internal conflict about what he has done. As Aristotle says, "their soul is divided against itself, and while one part, because of its wickedness, feels sorrow when it abstains from certain things, another part feels pleasure: one part pulls in one direction and the other in another as if to tear the individual to pieces . . . Bad people are full of regrets." (1166b19–24, Ostwald tr.)

Regardless of the plausibility of such views about wickedness, neither philosopher is particularly concerned with a man who *believes* that he is good but who is, in fact, fanatically wicked. Are there not

men who firmly believe that they are doing what is right when in fact their beliefs are pernicious? Consider the convinced Nazi or apartheid South African. Supposing there are such men, is it plausible to claim that independent of their beliefs about the moral value of their activities they are necessarily in a state of conflict? On the contrary, they seem to be identical psychologically with the virtuous man in that they do what they believe to be right. They act for the sake of principles, that is, they do what they do for its own sake and not for an ulterior purpose. Can they participate in the highest form of friend-ship?[8]

FOOTNOTES

1. A similar notion is found in *Republic* 352Dff., and in the Aristotelian works *Protrepticus*, fragment 6, and *Eudemian Ethics*, Bk. 2 Ch. 1.

2. Cf. *De Anima* Bk. 1 Ch. 5, and Bk. 2 Chs. 1, 2, 3.

3. Cf. *Protrepticus* Frag. 14W.

4. *'Ergon'* is sometimes translated 'function' and sometimes 'proper function.' Ross and Rackham are consistent in using 'function,' but Ostwald uses both, which is misleading. I shall use 'function' since 'proper' is worse than ambiguous. It might suggest 'unique' which, in the context would be pleonastic, and it might suggest 'morally appropriate' or 'beneficially appropriate' which in the context would be question begging.

5. "It is in the fulfillment of this function that a thing realizes what it truly is. . . ." Gauthier and Jolif, p. 55.

6. "one with high standards" (Ostwald). I will use 'good' as does Ross; it really doesn't matter which translation is used but 'good' suits my purposes, because it is clearer and shorter.

7. Could a man have wickedness as his aim? Cf. *Gorgias* 468C5–7, *Meno* 77B–78B, *Protagoras* 358C, where Socrates argues that nobody desires what is bad, which is interpreted by Socrates to mean 'evil' or 'wicked.' For a recent discussion of this issue in Plato, see "The Socratic Paradoxes" by Gerasimas Santas, *Philosophical Review*, April, 1964.

8. For a recent discussion of the rationality of immoralists and fanatics, see R. M. Hare, *Freedom and Reason*, Oxford, 1963.

THE NATURE OF AIMS*

John Dewey

Our problem now concerns the nature of ends, that is ends-in-view or aims. The essential elements in the problem have already been stated. It has been pointed out that the ends, objectives, of conduct are those foreseen consequences which influence present deliberation and which finally bring it to rest by furnishing an adequate stimulus to overt action. Consequently ends arise and function within action. They are not, as current theories too often imply, things lying beyond activity at which the latter is directed. They are not strictly speaking ends or termini of action at all. They are terminals of deliberation, and so turning points *in* activity. Many opposed moral theories agree however in placing ends beyond action, although they differ in their notions of what the ends are. The utilitarian sets up pleasure as such an outside-and-beyond, as something necessary to induce action and in which it terminates. Many harsh critics of utilitarianism have however agreed that there is some end in which action terminates, a final goal. They have denied that pleasure is such an outside aim, and put perfection or self-realization in its place. The entire popular notion of "ideals" is infected with this conception of some fixed end beyond activity at which we should aim. According to this view ends-in-themselves come before aims. We have a moral aim only as our purpose coincides with some end-in-itself. We *ought* to aim at the latter whether we actually do or not.

When men believed that fixed ends existed for all normal changes in nature, the conception of similar ends for men was but a special case of a general belief. If the changes in a tree from acorn to full-grown oak were regulated by an end which was somehow immanent or potential in all the less perfect forms, and if change was simply the effort to realize a perfect or complete form, then the acceptance of a like view for human conduct was consonant with the rest of what

* From John Dewey, *Human Nature and Conduct*, copyright 1922 by Henry Holt and Company; 1950 by John Dewey. Used by permission of Mrs. John Dewey and Holt, Rinehart and Winston, Inc., publishers.

passed for science. Such a view, consistent and systematic, was foisted by Aristotle upon western culture and endured for two thousand years. When the notion was expelled from natural science by the intellectual revolution of the seventeenth century, logically it should also have disappeared from the theory of human action. But man is not logical and his intellectual history is a record of mental reserves and compromises. He hangs on to what he can in his old beliefs even when he is compelled to surrender their logical basis. So the doctrine of fixed ends-in-themselves at which human acts are—or should be—directed and by which they are regulated if they are regulated at all persisted in morals, and was made the cornerstone of orthodox moral theory. The immediate effect was to dislocate moral from natural science, to divide man's world as it never had been divided in prior culture. One point of view, one method and spirit animated inquiry into natural occurrences; a radically opposite set of ideas prevailed about man's affairs. Completion of the scientific change begun in the seventeenth century thus depends upon a revision of the current notion of ends of action as fixed limits and conclusions.

In fact, ends are ends-in-view or aims. They arise out of natural effects or consequences which in the beginning are hit upon, stumbled upon so far as any purpose is concerned. Men *like* some of the consequences and *dislike* others. Henceforth (or till attraction and repulsion alter) attaining or averting similar consequences are aims or ends. These consequences constitute the meaning and value of an activity as it comes under deliberation. Meantime of course imagination is busy. Old consequences are enhanced, recombined, modified in imagination. Invention operates. Actual consequences, that is effects which have happened in the past, become possible future consequences of acts still to be performed. This operation of imaginative thought complicates the relation of ends to activity, but it does not alter the substantial fact: Ends are foreseen consequences which arise in the course of activity and which are employed to give activity added meaning and to direct its further course. They are in no sense ends *of* action. In being ends of *deliberation* they are redirecting pivots *in* action.

Men shoot and throw. At first this is done as an "instinctive" or natural reaction to some situation. The result when it is observed gives a new meaning to the activity. Henceforth men in throwing and shooting think of it in terms of its outcome; they act intelligently or have an end. Liking the activity in its acquired meaning, they not only "take aim" when they throw instead of throwing at random, but they

find or make targets at which to aim. This is the origin and nature of "goals" of action. They are ways of defining and deepening the meaning of activity. Having an end or aim is thus a characteristic of *present* activity. It is the means by which an activity becomes adapted when otherwise it would be blind and disorderly, or by which it gets meaning when otherwise it would be mechanical. In a strict sense an end-in-view is a *means* in present action; present action is not a means to a remote end. Men do not shoot because targets exist, but they set up targets in order that throwing and shooting may be more effective and significant.

A mariner does not sail towards the stars, but by noting the stars he is aided in conducting his present activity of sailing. A port or harbor is his objective, but only in the sense of *reaching* it not of taking possession of it. The harbor stands in this thought as a significant point at which his activity will need re-direction. Activity will not cease when the port is attained, but merely the *present direction* of activity. The port is as truly the beginning of another mode of activity as it is the termination of the present one. The only reason we ignore this fact is because it is empirically taken for granted. We know without thinking that our "ends" are perforce beginnings. But theories of ends and ideals have converted a theoretical ignoring which is equivalent to practical acknowledgment into an intellectual denial, and have thereby confused and perverted the nature of ends.

Even the most important among all the consequences of an act is not necessarily its aim. Results which are objectively most important may not even be thought of at all; ordinarily a man does not think in connection with exercise of his profession that it will sustain him and his family in existence. The end-thought-of is uniquely important, but it is indispensable to state the respect in which it is important. It gives the decisive clew to the act to be performed under the existing circumstances. It is that particular foreseen object that will stimulate the act which relieves existing troubles, straightens out existing entanglements. In a temporary annoyance, even if only that caused by the singing of a mosquito, the thought of that which gives relief may engross the mind in spite of consequences much more important, objectively speaking. Moralists have deplored such facts as evidence of levity. But the remedy, if a remedy be needed, is not found in insisting upon the importance of ends in general. It is found in a change of the dispositions which make things either immediately troublesome or tolerable or agreeable.

When ends are regarded as literally ends to action rather than as

directive stimuli to present choice they are frozen and isolated. It makes no difference whether the "end" is a "natural" good like health or a "moral" good like honesty. Set up as complete and exclusive, as demanding and justifying action as a means to itself, it leads to narrowness; in extreme cases fanaticism, inconsiderateness, arrogance and hypocrisy. Joshua's reputed success in getting the sun to stand still to serve his desire is recognized to have involved a miracle. But moral theorists constantly assume that the continuous course of events can be arrested at the point of a particular object; that men can plunge with their own desires into the unceasing flow of changes, and seize upon some object as their end irrespective of everything else. The use of intelligence to discover the object that will best operate as a releasing and unifying stimulus in the existing situation is discounted. One reminds one's self that one's end is justice or charity or professional achievement or putting over a deal for a needed public improvement, and further questionings and qualms are stilled.

It is customary to suppose that such methods merely ignore the question of the morality of the means which are used to secure the end desired. Common sense revolts against the maxim, conveniently laid off upon Jesuits or other far-away people, that the end justifies the means. There is no incorrectness in saying that the question of means employed is overlooked in such cases. But analysis would go further if it were also pointed out that overlooking means is only a device for failing to note those ends, or consequences, which, if they were noted would be seen to be so evil that action would be estopped. Certainly nothing can justify or condemn means except ends, results. But we have to include consequences impartially. Even admitting that lying will save a man's soul, whatever that may mean, it would still be true that lying will have other consequences, namely, the usual consequences that follow from tampering with good faith and that lead lying to be condemned. It is wilful folly to fasten upon some single end or consequence which is liked, and permit the view of that to blot from perception all other undesired and undesirable consequences. It is like supposing that when a finger held close to the eye covers up a distant mountain the finger is really larger than the mountain. Not *the* end—in the singular—justifies the means; for there is no such thing as the single all-important end. To suppose that there is such an end is like working over again, in behalf of our private wishes, the miracle of Joshua in arresting the course of nature. It is not possible adequately to characterize the presumption, the falsity and the deliberate perversion of intelligence involved in refusal to note the plural effects that flow

from any act, a refusal adopted in order that we may justify an act by picking out that one consequence which will enable us to do what we wish to do and for which we feel the need of justification.

Yet this assumption is continually made. It is made by implication in the current view of purposes or ends-in-view as objects in themselves, instead of means to unification and liberation of present conflicting, confused habits and impulses. There is something almost sinister in the desire to label the doctrine that the end justifies the means with the name of some one obnoxious school. Politicians, especially if they have to do with the foreign affairs of a nation and are called statesmen, almost uniformly act upon the doctrine that the welfare of their own country justifies any measure irrespective of all the demoralization it works. Captains of industry, great executives in all lines, usually work upon this plan. But they are not the original offenders by any means. Every man works upon it so far as he permits himself to become so absorbed in one aspect of what he is doing that he loses a view of its varied consequences, hypnotizing his attention by consideration of just those consequences which in the abstract are desirable and slurring over other consequences equally real. Every man works upon this principle who becomes over-interested in any cause or project, and who uses its desirability in the abstract to justify himself in employing any means that will assist him in arriving, ignoring all the collateral "ends" of his behavior. It is frequently pointed out that there is a type of executive-man whose conduct seems to be as non-moral as the action of the forces of nature. We all tend to relapse into this non-moral condition whenever we want any one thing intensely. In general, the identification of the end prominent in conscious desire and effort with *the* end is part of the technique of avoiding a reasonable survey of consequences. The survey is avoided because of a subconscious recognition that it would reveal desire in its true worth and thus preclude action to satisfy it—or at all events give us an uneasy conscience in striving to realize it. Thus the doctrine of the isolated, complete or fixed end limits intelligent examination, encourages insincerity, and puts a pseudo-stamp of moral justification upon success at any price.

Moralistic persons are given to escaping this evil by falling into another pit. They deny that consequences have anything at all to do with the morality of acts. Not ends but motives they say justify or condemn acts. The thing to do, accordingly, is to cultivate certain motives or dispositions, benevolence, purity, love of perfection, loyalty. The denial of consequence thus turns out formal, verbal. In reality a

consequence is set up at which to aim, only it is a subjective consequence. "Meaning well" is selected as *the* consequence or end to be cultivated at all hazards, an end which is all-justifying and to which everything else is offered up in sacrifice. The result is a sentimental futile com-
placency rather than the brutal efficiency of the executive. But the root
of both evils is the same. One man selects some external consequence, the
other man a state of internal feeling, to serve as the end. The doctrine of
meaning well as *the* end is if anything the more contemptible of
the two, for it shrinks from accepting any responsibility for actual results. It is negative, self-protective and sloppy. It leads itself to complete
self-deception.

Why have men become so attached to fixed, external ends? Why
is it not universally recognized that an end is a device of intelligence in
guiding action, instrumental to freeing and harmonizing troubled and
divided tendencies? The answer is virtually contained in what was
earlier said about rigid habits and their effect upon intelligence. Ends
are, in fact, literally endless, forever coming into existence as new
activities occasion new consequences. "Endless ends" is a way of
saying that there are no ends—that is no fixed self-enclosed finalities.
While however we cannot actually prevent change from occurring we
can and do regard it as evil. We strive to retain action in ditches
already dug. We regard novelties as dangerous, experiments as illicit
and deviations as forbidden. Fixed and separate ends reflect a projec-
tion of our own fixed and non-interacting compartmental habits. We
see only consequences which correspond to our habitual courses. As
we have said, men did not begin to shoot because there were ready-
made targets to aim at. They made things into targets by shooting at
them, and then made special targets to make shooting more signifi-
cantly interesting. But if generation after generation were shown
targets they had had no part in constructing, if bows and arrows were
thrust into their hands, and pressure were brought to bear upon them
to keep them shooting in season and out, some wearied soul would
soon propound to willing listeners the theory that shooting was un-
natural, that man was naturally wholly at rest, and that targets existed
in order that men might be forced to be active; that the duty of
shooting and the virtue of hitting are externally imposed and fostered,
and that otherwise there would be no such thing as a shooting-activity
—that is, morality.

The doctrine of fixed ends not only diverts attention from examination of consequences and the intelligent creation of purpose, but,
since means and ends are two ways of regarding the same actuality, it

also renders men careless in their inspection of existing conditions. An aim not framed on the basis of a survey of those present conditions which are to be employed as means of its realization simply throws us back upon past habits. We then do not do what we intended to do but what we have got used to doing, or else we thrash about in a blind ineffectual way. The result is failure. Discouragement follows, assuaged perhaps by the thought that in any case the end is too ideal, too noble and remote, to be capable of realization. We fall back on the consoling thought that our moral ideals are too good for this world and that we must accustom ourselves to a gap between aim and execution. Actual life is then thought of as a compromise with the best, an enforced second or third best, a dreary exile from our true home in the ideal, or a temporary period of troubled probation to be followed by a period of unending attainment and peace. At the same time, as has been repeatedly pointed out, persons of a more practical turn of mind accept the world "as it is," that is as past customs have made it to be, and consider what advantages for themselves may be extracted from it. They form aims on the basis of existing habits of life which may be turned to their own private account. They employ intelligence in framing ends and selecting and arranging means. But intelligence is confined to manipulation; it does not extend to construction. It is the intelligence of the politician, administrator and professional executive —the kind of intelligence which has given a bad meaning to a word that ought to have a fine meaning, opportunism. For the highest task of intelligence is to grasp and realize genuine opportunity, possibility.

Roughly speaking, the course of forming aims is as follows. The beginning is with a wish, an emotional reaction against the present state of things and a hope for something different. Action fails to connect satisfactorily with surrounding conditions. Thrown back upon itself, it projects itself in an imagination of a scene which if it were present would afford satisfaction. This picture is often called an aim, more often an ideal. But in itself it is a fancy which may be only a phantasy, a dream, a castle in the air. In itself it is a romantic embellishment of the present; at its best it is material for poetry or the novel. Its natural home is not in the future but in the dim past or in some distant and supposedly better part of the present world. Every such idealized object is suggested by something actually experienced, as the flight of birds suggests the liberation of human beings from the restrictions of slow locomotion on dull earth. It becomes an aim or end only when it is worked out in terms of concrete conditions available for its realization, that is in terms of "means."

This transformation depends upon study of the conditions which generate or make possible the fact observed to exist already. The fancy of the delight of moving at will through the air became an actuality only after men carefully studied the way in which a bird although heavier than air actually sustains itself in air. A fancy becomes an aim, in short, when some past sequence of known cause-and-effect is projected into the future, and when by assembling its casual conditions we strive to generate a like result. We have to fall back upon what has already happened naturally without design, and study it to see *how* it happened, which is what is meant by causation. This knowledge joined to wish creates a purpose. Many men have doubtless dreamed of ability to have light in darkness without the trouble of oil, lamps and friction. Glow-worms, lightning, the sparks of cut electric conductors suggest such a possibility. But the picture remained a dream until an Edison studied all that could be found out about such casual phenomena of light, and then set to work to search out and gather together the means for reproducing their operation. The great trouble with what passes for moral ends and ideals is that they do not get beyond the stage of fancy of something agreeable and desirable based upon an emotional wish; very often, at that, not even an original wish, but the wish of some leader which has been conventionalized and transmitted through channels of authority. Every gain in natural science makes possible new aims. That is, the discovery of how things *do* occur makes it possible to conceive of their happening at will, and gives us a start on selecting and combining the conditions, the means, to command their happening. In technical matters, this lesson has been fairly well learned. But in moral matters, men still largely neglect the need of studying the way in which results similar to those which we desire actually happen. Mechanism is despised as of importance only in low material things. The consequent divorce of moral ends from scientific study of natural events renders the former impotent wishes, compensatory dreams in consciousness. In *fact* ends or consequences are still determined by fixed habit and the force of circumstance. The evils of idle dreaming and of routine are experienced in conjunction. "Idealism" must indeed come first—the imagination of some better state generated by desire. But unless ideals are to be dreams and idealism a synonym for romanticism and phantasy-building, there must be a most realistic study of actual conditions and of the mode or law of natural events, in order to give the imagined or ideal object definite form and solid substance—to give it, in short, practicality and constitute it a working end.

THOUGHT AND ACTION IN ARISTOTLE*

G. E. M. Anscombe

✤

Is Aristotle inconsistent in the different things he says about *prohairesis*, mostly translated "choice," in the different parts of the *Ethics?* The following seems to be a striking inconsistency. In Book III (1113a 4) he says that what is "decided by deliberation" is chosen (*to ek tes boulesis krithen prohaireton estin*), but he also often insists that the uncontrolled man, the *akrates*, does not *choose* to do what he does; that is to say, what he does in doing the kind of thing that he disapproves of, is not what Aristotle will call exercising choice; the uncontrolled man does not act from choice, *ek prohaireseos*, or choosing, *prohairoumenos*. However, in Book VI (1142b 18) he mentions the possibility of a calculating uncontrolled man who will get what he arrived at by calculation, *ek tou logismou teuxetai*, and so will have deliberated correctly: *orthos estai bebouleumenos*. Thus we have the three theses: (*a*) choice is what is determined by deliberation; (*b*) what the uncontrolled man does *qua* uncontrolled, he does not choose to do; (*c*) the uncontrolled man, even when acting against his convictions, does on occasion determine what to do by deliberation.

Without a doubt the set of passages is inconsistent if we are to understand that any case of something being determined by deliberation at all is a case of choice, as seems to be suggested by the formulation "what is decided by deliberation is chosen."

If, then, Aristotle is consistent, perhaps his "choice" is not *simply* determination by calculating or deliberating. There is some reason to think this; though he says that what is determined by deliberation (*krithen ek tes boules*) *is* chosen, we may say that the *context* shows that he himself has in mind a deliberation what to do with a view to one's ends, and that ends are things like being honoured, health, the life of virtue, or of material prosperity, enjoyment of knowledge or

* Reprinted from R. Bambrough, ed., *New Essays on Plato and Aristotle*, New York, 1965, by permission of the author, The Humanities Press, and Routledge & Kegan Paul Ltd.

sensual pleasure. The uncontrolled man, the *akrates*, is not one whose general object is, say, enjoying a life of sensual pleasure; he simply has the *particular* purpose of seducing his neighbour's wife.

On this view, we remove the inconsistency by saying that "choice" is of something determined not just by any deliberation, but by deliberation how to obtain an object of one's *will* (*boulesis*) rather than merely of one's *desire* (*epithumia*): there will be a contrast here even for the *akolastos*, the licentious man. For *his* will is *to satisfy his desires, his sensual appetites;* and his decision to seduce his neighbour's wife, say, is a "choice," as well as being an expression of his lusts, just because his end in life *is* to satisfy his lusts; this has to be shown before one can say that a man who is going after objects of "desire" evilly, has a bad "choice."

Now—though I think this does represent Aristotle's view—an objection that strikes one is that people's "ends" aren't in general nearly as definitely one thing or another as Aristotle makes out. If "will" (*boulesis*) is simply the type of wanting (*orexis*) that one has in relation to one's final objective *in* what one is deliberately doing at any time, then there seems no objection to saying that the weak man at 1151a 2 (the uncontrolled man who calculates how to get what tempts him, for he is surely a man of the weak rather than the impulsive type) has a *will* to seduce his neighbour's wife, or a will for the pleasure of it, at the time when he is cleverly reckoning how to do it. The fact that he has a bad conscience about it doesn't seem to be either here or there *for determining whether he is making that his aim* for the time being; but this fact, that he has a bad conscience about it, *is* just what makes him uncontrolled rather than licentious, *akrates* rather than *akolastos*.

There is, however, another defence against the charge of inconsistency, which perhaps is not open to the objection that it requires an unrealistic idea of the clearcutness of people's ends. Not all deliberation is with a view to making a "choice," forming a *prohairesis*, where none has yet been made; some deliberation is with a view to executing a "choice." This is made clear at 1144a 20; "Virtue makes one's choice right, but as for what has to be done for the sake of it, that doesn't belong to virtue but to another power—cleverness." *Ten men oun prohairesin orthen poiei he arete. To d'hosa ekeines heneka prattesthai ouk esti tes aretes all'heteras dunameos.*

But also in Book III Aristotle speaks of *trying* to do the thing that a deliberation has terminated in: "if it seems possible, they try to do it. Possible things are the things that *might* come about through us" (1112b 26). So we might say that something that seems to be a way of

achieving your end and to be possible may be decided upon; *that* you will do this (or at least will try) is a "choice;" and now there may be further deliberation just how to manage that possible-seeming thing. Now in Book III there is no suggestion that wanting (*orexis* of) the more immediate means (adopted to execute the remoter means that have already been decided on) is not itself *also* a "choice," *prohairesis*. But if we are to reconcile the denial (which *also* occurs in Book III 1111b 14) that the uncontrolled man acts *choosing* so to act (*prohairoumenos*) with the account in Book VI of a calculating uncontrolled man, then we must say that when deliberation how to execute a decision terminates in an action—the man contrives a skilful approach to the woman—this will not be a case of "choice" if the decision was not reached by deliberation.

Thus the passages in which Aristotle describes deliberation as going on till we have reached something we can do here and now, and describes "choice" as being of what deliberation has reached, must not lead us to think that matter for a "choice" has *only* been reached when there is no more room for deliberation of any kind.

On the other hand, just as the first defence left us wondering what Aristotle supposed a *boulesis*, a case of "will," to be, since apparently the pleasure sought by the uncontrolled man who calculates is not an object of his will; so this defence leaves us in the dark as to what a "choice" is. We may well have thought we knew this; for "what you can do here and now, which you have reached as a result of deliberating how to achieve an end"—the first cause (*proton aition*), the last thing in analysis and first in execution—did seem a relatively clear notion. But if, as must be admitted on the basis of the text, there is room for calculating how to execute a "choice," then just where in the chain of deliberations from an end to the immediate thing that I can do without having to consider *how* to do it—just where in this chain does the first "choice" come?

It must be admitted that Aristotle's account of deliberation (*bouleusis*, or *boule*) often seems to fit deliberation about how to execute a decision, and in particular to fit technical deliberation, better than deliberation which is about the means here and now to "living well in general"—*pros to cu zen holos*. It seems at its clearest when he is describing the doctor deliberating how to restore health by reducing the imbalance of humours by . . . , etc. But this is a piece of technical deliberation.

I am not saying that Aristotle so uses "*prohairesis*" ("choice") that the termination of a piece of technical deliberation isn't a "choice."

The acceptance of fixed ends in themselves is an aspect of man's devotion to an ideal of certainty. This affection was inevitably cherished as long as men believed that the highest things in physical nature are at rest, and that science is possible only by grasping immutable forms and species: in other words, for much the greater part of the intellectual history of mankind. Only reckless sceptics would have dared entertain any idea of ends except as fixed in themselves as long as the whole structure of science was erected upon the immobile. Behind however the conception of fixity whether in science or morals lay adherence to certainty of "truth," a clinging to something fixed, born of fear of the new and of attachment to possessions. When the classicist condemns concession to impulse and holds up to admiration the patterns tested in tradition, he little suspects how much he is himself affected by unavowed impulses—timidity which makes him cling to authority, conceit which moves him to be himself the authority who speaks in the name of authority, possessive impulse which fears to risk acquisition in new adventures. Love of certainty is a demand for guarantees in advance of action. Ignoring the fact that truth can be bought only by the adventure of experiment, dogmatism turns truth into an insurance company. Fixed ends upon one side and fixed "principles"—that is authoritative rules—on the other, are props for a feeling of safety, the refuge of the timid and the means by which the bold prey upon the timid.

On the contrary; that would, I think, be quite inconsistent with the treatment in Book III. But Book VI teaches us, as I think we might not have realised from Book III, that there is no such thing as a "choice" which is *only* technical (I use "technical" to cover practical cleverness in bringing particular situations about, even when it's not strictly a technique that's in question). There is always, on Aristotle's view, another "choice" behind a technical or purely executive one (1139b 1–3). That is why he denies the name of *"prohairesis"*, "choice," to the technical or executive decision, even though this is the fruit of deliberation, if that particular thing for the sake of which this decision is being made is not *itself* decided upon by deliberation.

To return to the weak, calculating, uncontrolled man, who disapproves of adultery but is tempted about his neighbour's wife: he gives way to the temptation and sets out to seduce her; then he calculates how best to do this and shows plenty of cleverness in his calculations. If he had been a licentious man, an *akolastos*, the decision to seduce her would have been a "choice," and the volition to perform each of the steps that he reckoned would enable him to succeed would in turn each have been a "choice" too. For the decision to seduce this woman was simply the particular application of his general policy of pursuing sensual enjoyment. But although the uncontrolled man perhaps reckons how to proceed—once he has given way to the temptation to go after this woman—in exactly the same way as the licentious man, his volitions in performing the steps that he calculates will enable him to succeed are not "choices." (Aristotle, of course, does not set up a word for "volition" as I have been using it.) So we have to say that the uncontrolled man carries out a deliberation how to execute what would have been a "choice" if he had been an *akolastos;* this, however, is something for which Aristotle has no regular name—for he has no general use of a psychological verb or abstract noun corresponding to *"hekousion"* (usually translated "voluntary") as *"prohaireisthai"* ("choose"), *"prohairesis"* ("choice"), correspond to *"prohaireton"* ("chosen"). Of course he regards the uncontrolled man as acting voluntarily. When he describes this man as calculating cleverly, he says he will get what he "proposes" (*protithetai*); and this verb expresses a volition, or perhaps rather an intention. Aristotle ought, we may say, to have seen that he was here employing a key concept in the theory of action, but he did not do so; the innocent unnoticeable verb he uses receives no attention from him.

Let us return to the point that a technical "choice" is never the only "choice" that is made by the man who makes it. The definition of

"choice" as *orexis bouleutike*—deliberative wanting—would not at first sight seem to justify this. The calculating uncontrolled man choosing means of seduction—he wants them, surely, i.e., has an *orexis* for them, and this is a result of deliberation. However, there is—what may give us pause in making this criticism—a puzzling remark in that passage in Book VI (1139a 17–b 13) where Aristotle devotes most discussion to this definition of "choice." He says ". . . choice does not exist without intellect and judgment, *nor yet without* moral character." *out aneu nou kai dianoias out aneu ethikes estin hexeos he prohairesis.* That sentence, in fact, starts with the word *"dio"*—"That is why." It is puzzling, because while the previous sentences give ample grounds for saying that choice involves intelligence, they don't seem to give any ground for saying that it involves moral character. However, the succeeding sentence starts "For"—so perhaps we should look for the explanation there first. "For doing well, and its opposite, does not exist without judgment and character." *eupraxia gar kai to enantion en praxei aneu dianoias kai ethous ouk estin.* That does not seem to help us much. A little farther on, however, he tells us "The end, absolutely speaking, is not anything one *makes*, but something one *does*. For doing well is the end, and that is the object of the wanting (*he d'orexis toutou*). That is why choice is appetitive (*orektike*) intelligence or intelligent wanting."

This brings us back to our first defence; namely, that something is only a "choice" if it is of means to the objects of a man's "will" (*boulesis*); hence, however much calculation may have gone into determining it, if it is of what is only a means to the objects of a man's *epithumiai*, his "desires," then unless his "will" in life *is* to satisfy these desires (as holds of the licentious man) it is not a "choice." Thus the second defence resolves into the first. The second defence was that since some deliberation is done with a view to executing a "choice," something may be reached as a result of deliberation even when the significant decision what to do has already been made; and if this has *not* been made by deliberation (*krithen ek tes boules*), then it was not a "choice," and the results of deliberations how to execute it won't be "choices" either. Well, the question whether the significant decision is reached by deliberation seems to reduce to the question whether it is made with a view to the objects of the man's "will" (*boulesis*). Now our question about this was: what does Aristotle suppose "will" (*boulesis*) to be? Why, we asked, shouldn't we say that the uncontrolled man has a "will" for the pleasure he hopes to obtain from seducing his neighbour's wife? The answer we get suggested by the

passage in Book VI is: the uncontrolled man is not prepared to say: "This is my idea of good work (*eupraxia*), this is the kind of life I want." Whereas, of course, that is the attitude of the licentious man, the *akolastos:* a life spent doing such things is his idea of a well-spent life—and a fig for moral virtue. It is not that the licentious man thinks licentiousness is moral virtue; what he thinks is rather that this is a good way to carry on. "One should pursue the present pleasure," *dei to paron hedu diokein,* doesn't mean: it's virtuous, or morally obligatory, to do that—but: that's the thing to do!

Now, why can't one have "choice" without moral character of some sort? I think Aristotle does not explain this, beyond saying that "doing well," "a good way of carrying on" is the end of any "choice;" i.e., any sort of decision which does not have in view what one thinks of as a good way of proceeding in one's life, does *not* qualify to be a "choice."

His thesis, then, clearly is that there is no such thing as your acting with *eupraxia,* "doing well," in view unless you have some sort of moral character, virtuous or vicious. Now, how is this? Let us imagine some cases.

Someone thinks that it is a good sort of life always to get the better of people by tricking them, taking them in, defrauding them; to do that is to be strong and not soft and not a sucker oneself, and to get the best of whatever's going; whereas the honest man is weak and soft and a fool, and always gets the worst of things. A particular decision to cheat X will be a "choice" of something here and now which he makes for the sake of doing well as he conceives it.

Another case: Someone thinks that he will do well if he spends his life in scientific research; to do this he must have leisure; to get the money for his living expenses he does a disgraceful but not time-consuming thing: one great fraud.

These are two rather different types of case; however, in both of them it would be natural enough to say that the man is described as having a sort of moral character. On Aristotle's view, a character exists only when there is an habitual performance of the typical acts of that character. Now I have described the cases so that the men's ends are clear, but I have put in only one act for each. The first case is not credibly described on the supposition that there is only one such act. This one act with a view to this sort of "doing well"—what is supposed to have preceded it? Has he done things of the same sort, but not done them under any such conception? under what conception, then?—say in obedience to a mentor, or attracted by the particular

gains of each action? Very well; but what is to make us call this the first act done with a view to that sort of "doing well"? It is not enough for the agent to have those thoughts; suppose he had them on just one occasion—that would not show that he was acting so as to "do well" in that kind of way, only that he had indulged in a certain picture of his actions. Only if they are the thoughts which come to habitually inspire those actions shall we be able to say: that is his end, that is his idea of a good way of going on. If, on the other hand, he had not done any actions of the sort before, then still more one would want plenty of actions performed under the influence of his new thoughts before one could recognise one as done with a view to this sort of "doing well" rather than as, say, an experiment in wrongdoing.

The other case is different; here the single act which is to be the object of a choice is not the kind of act which the agent supposes to be the way to spend his life well. If the agent had never done any scientific research or study at all, then the description of the case would be suspect. Either it would be nonsense, or it would be a description of someone under a fantastic illusion. Perhaps it is possible to conceive something as the activity you aim to spend your life at even though you never do it at all, even in a feeble and elementary fashion. But then either it would have to be something you could understand without doing it (like riding horses, say), or you could only want the name, no doubt with some piece of imagination attached —as if, e.g., someone who had never learnt any mathematics wanted to become a mathematician because of the expression on the face of a mathematician he knew, and had no other conception of a good way of spending his life: that was it, for him. This would rather be a lunatic obsession than a conception of a certain sort of doing well as the end.

If, then, "choice" is only of those things which are done as means to "doing well," we may concede that Aristotle is right in saying that it does not occur without moral character, i.e., without good or bad habitual action. But there is no reason to say that the action which is the subject of "choice" must itself be the act of a virtue or a vice. That will only be so where the objects of "choice" are (in Greenwood's phrase) constitutive means towards the (putative) good way of going on. In the second case I described, the fraudulent act was a productive means; and if the man did not perform other fraudulent acts, this act would not mean that he was a fraudulent man—i.e., that he had the vice of being fraudulent.

The notion of "choice" as conceived by Aristotle, his *prohairesis*,

is a very peculiar one. I used to think it spurious. If it had been a winner, like some other Aristotelian concepts, would not "proheretic" be a word as familiar to us as "practical" is?

At any rate, "choice" cannot do all the work Aristotle wants to make it do. The uncontrolled man who has further intentions in doing what he does, whose actions are deliberate, although the deliberation is in the interests of a desire which conflicts with what he regards as doing well—to describe his action we need a concept (our "intention") having to do with will or appetition: not just *epithumia*, "desire," for that may be only a feeling.

Aristotle talks as if "desire" were a force (1147a 34), but this is only a metaphor. He will have it that if one acts against one's convictions, one's judgment has always failed in some way under the influence of "desire" or some other passion. One fails to know or remember either the last premise or, possibly, the conclusion. There are such cases. For example, a man who disapproves of adultery may fail to find out something which he easily could have found out, and so may commit adultery through culpable ignorance of a particular premise: "This woman, whom I have picked up at a party, is someone's wife"— his failure to find out being explained by his passion. And similarly for failure to get or keep clear before one's mind already known facts, with their implications for action in view of one's ends; and for lies one may tell inwardly or outwardly when one wants to do wrong. But Aristotle writes as if these were the only cases of doing what you believe is wrong. He apparently cannot admit the case where a person forms a perfectly clear-headed intention of acting contrary to his convictions. On one interpretation the trouble always concerns one of the particular premises; on another, Aristotle allows a case where the sinner is clear about all these, but then fails to draw the conclusion; at most he draws it verbally, without knowledge of what he is saying.

The usual explanations of this are that Aristotle was a Greek, that he was still under Plato's influence, etc. No doubt there is something in that; particularly when he restricts the explanation "he repeats the thing, but it's just babble like a drunk man reciting Empedocles" to the particular premise: or possibly to that and the conclusion. It is, surely an explanation far better suited to enunciation of the universal premise, say: "No one should commit adultery" or "It is disgraceful to get very drunk," by the man who is about to do it. Aristotle explicitly wants to exempt the universal sort of knowledge from "being dragged about like a slave."

However, I suspect that he was also influenced by his own

conception of practical reasoning. To set out the form of practical reasoning is to set out the form of deliberation (*bouleusis*). If it is all made explicit (as of course it hardly would be in real life, since one does not need to advert to the obvious) its formal character becomes quite clear. You have a set of premises starting with a universal one to the effect that a kind of thing A is, say, profitable for a kind of being B, and proceeding through intermediate premises like "C's are A's" and "a C can be obtained by a procedure D" and "a procedure D can be carried out by doing E," together with another premise to the effect that you are, or someone whose profit is your concern is, a B; and if the action E is something that you can do, then it is clear that the conclusion of this reasoning is for you to do E. But let us consider what this means. Does it mean that if you have embarked on the reasoning you *must* do E? Aristotle seems to have thought so. At least he thought you must do E unless something prevented you—the something might be the drive of "desire," *epithumia, against* doing E. When making this point, he often gave examples of practical syllogisms in which there is a certain necessity about the conclusion.—"It is necessary to taste everything sweet, and this is sweet" (1147a 29); "Every man must walk, and I am a man;" "Now no man must walk, and I am a man." The last two examples come from the *Movement of Animals*, Chapter VII. The man does the thing in question (walks or halts) at once, if not prevented from walking in the one case, or forced to walk in the other. There are two features suggesting the necessity of the conclusion—the gerundive form, and the type of universality in the premise.

> Every man has got to walk
> I am a man
> I have got to walk

is a formally valid deductive argument—I will call such an argument a proof-syllogism. I mean that it is a proof of the conclusion, if only the premises are true. Now Aristotle had special ideas about proof, so he would not have agreed to say what I have just said. "Every man has got to walk" is not a changeless truth, so he would have said this is not apodeictic (see, e.g., 1040a 33–5). Disregarding this let us merely note the formal validity of the reasoning as a deduction. Further, let us grant that if I agree to the premises and therefore to the conclusion, and say "I have got to walk," speaking quite seriously, it would be queer of me not to walk, if nothing prevented me.

Now let us look at another example:

I need a covering,
A cloak is a covering,
I need a cloak;
I must make what I need,
I need a cloak,
I must make a cloak.

The conclusion, that a cloak must be made, Aristotle says, *is* an action: *to sumperasma to himation poieteon praxis esti.* So here is a "choice." But, he goes on, action has a starting point—and so he sketches the reasoning with a view to execution of the "choice": "If there's to be a cloak, first such and such is needed, and if such and such, so and so," *ei himation estai ananke tode proton, ei de tode, tode* and this last the man does at once. Now it is hard to tell whether Aristotle reflected that "I need a cloak" is not a formally valid deductive conclusion from "I need a covering and a cloak is a covering." The fact that it is not, is, I should contend, no criticism of the syllogism as a piece of practical reasoning. But it is possible that if he had been challenged about this, he would have said one could amend the syllogism by putting in that a cloak was the best covering or the easiest to make or something of that sort. (Cf. *Nicomachean Ethics* 1112b 16.) For he is marked by an anxiety to make practical reasoning out to be as like as possible to speculative reasoning. "They work just the same," he says in the *Movement of Animals, eoike paraplesios sumbainein,* and seems to be referring to a necessitation of the conclusion. But you do not get this where various ways of obtaining the end are possible.

A further sign is that when he is looking at practical syllogism in this light—as necessarily yielding the conclusion—his examples of the first universal premises always go "It's needed," "It's expedient," "such and such a kind of being ought to do such and such a kind of thing." He wants a "must" in the conclusion in the verbalised form in which he gives it in the *Movement of Animals,* though each time he gives the conclusion he adds—"and that's an action." But when he is not talking about this automatic-machine aspect of the practical syllogism—which he is keen on because he thinks it helps to make it clear how the syllogism *kinei,* how it sets the human animal in motion—then we have such a universal premise as "Heavy waters are unwholesome." Here the *De Anima* formulation (of a doctrine also expressed in the *Nicomachean Ethics* at 1040b 16, though not so clearly) that the starting-

point of the whole business is what you want (the *arche* is the *orekton*) can come into play. And we may remark that there are two possible conclusions of the reasoning about heavy waters, according as you want to be healthy or not. That, of course, sounds absurd; but let the universal be "Strong alkalis are deadly poison," and it is easy to spell out the practical reasoning of the suicide. Aristotle recognises this two-way possibility at *Metaphysics* IX, 1046b 5–7.

It looks as if, in his enthusiasm for making practical reasoning like theoretical and explaining its power to set one in motion (aided, no doubt, by his own picture of proof and by the Platonic conception of sin as error, which he did not entirely shake off), Aristotle did not notice some significant features of his discovery; the fact that though it is perfectly correct to call practical reasoning "reasoning," and though some practical syllogisms are also (in my sense) proof syllogisms, i.e. are entailments, in general practical syllogisms have a different form from proof syllogisms.

Consider:

Owning a Launderette would make me wealthy.
There is scope for opening a Launderette on such-and-such premises.

and so on down to where I might get going. This is practical reasoning, and given all the premises it is a formal matter what the conclusion is, in the form "so I'll. . . ." Whether, if it is I who have put out the syllogism, I *draw* the conclusion, depends on whether I actively want to be wealthy and am working out this one of the many possibilities with a view to action—I might be doing it idly, or as an academic example. If by a practical syllogism you mean—as Aristotle did (*De Anima* 433 a 15)—one that terminates in action, and the purpose of which is to act, then this won't be practical; but if you mean a *type* of reasoning—i.e., reasoning reaching from a general sort of objective to something one can choose to do here and now—then it will be practical (St. Thomas would call it "theoretical *de practicis*" (*Summa Theologica* IQ. 14 art. 16c.). In general, people would not trouble to work such things out except with a view to action.

We have seen two strands in Aristotle's thought. First there is the explanation of how the human being is set in motion by thought, and second there is the idea of the thing wanted as the starting-point for such thought. For the first he seems to have wanted, not only a necessity in the connections which is not always present in practical reasonings, but also a compulsiveness about the universal premise, a

"must" about it: that is, it seems he wanted a universal premise acceptance of which implies intellectual acknowledgment of it as the guide to action. The need for necessity in the connections can fairly be discounted. Then we can happily combine the two strands by postulating at the back of all these premises a first premise to the effect that only such-and-such is doing well, is happiness or blessedness, "the good for man." Aristotle's grand universal premise is that blessedness is activity in accordance with virtue, especially intellectual virtue. The argument for this as the true premise is the *Nicomachean Ethics* itself. If the truth of this premise is acknowledged, then it is itself acknowledged as the ultimate guide to action. For blessedness, or doing well, is the end that anyone must have so far as he has a rational end, that is to say so far as he has "will," i.e., the kind of wanting that belongs in the rational part, at all. (Cf. *De Anima* 432b 5–7.)

Here we touch on the difference between Aristotle and Hume. Hume's doctrine that reason is inert, that for considerations to lead to any action a sentiment, a passion, is required may be compared to Aristotle's "It is not reason as such that sets in motion; but reason which is with a view to something and is practical" (1139a 36). Aristotle's "will" will then be a "calm passion" in Hume's terminology. But they disagree about the applicability of the descriptions "in accordance with reason" and "not in accordance with reason" to actions and wants.

I suggest that the idea of rational wanting should be explained in terms of what is wanted being wanted *qua* conducive to or part of "doing well," or blessedness. If one admits that what one wants is no good, but still one wants it, it is, in Aristotle's conception, merely the object of a passion; when the thing that one so wants is a pleasure, though it is no good (like smoking in some people's view) then one is being led simply by "desire," *epithumia*. For though what constitutes blessedness is necessarily utterly pleasant, it is not something one wants because it is a pleasure even though it should be no good; on the contrary, it is the object of will as the best possible thing for a human being, being the activity of his rational part and the activity that is an end, not a means.

For as seeing can be seen to be what the eye is for, so understanding—the enjoyment of the truth—can be seen to be what the mind is for. But here we must note a certain split in Aristotle's thought. For the highest blessedness he thought of as something divine, which we should grasp at to the poor extent that we can—taking the side of and imitating the immortal. He coins a word for what we should do, namely "to immortalize" (*athanatizein* 1177b 33), sounding like an

echo of "to Medize" which means to be on the side of and imitate the Persian. But he acknowledges that in the ordinary course of life for most people "doing well" amounts to something more mundane: a successful and honourable conduct of life, the heart of which is, if one judges rightly, action in accordance with *moral* virtue.

Apart from being ruled by passion (this is what I want, even if it is no good) "doing well" is what anyone wants in some obscure and indeterminate way. One could call it that part of blessedness for which one's own action is essential. Aristotle's unrealistic conception of the clearcutness of people's ends seems on investigation not to be so bad as it looked. For the many objectives that are no good, and aren't thought of as being good, are allowed for in his thought. The assumption of clearcutness is the assumption that people generally know what they count as "doing well"—i.e., that they definitely so count being rich or being famous or the life of knowledge.

My eventual goal has been to expound the concept of "practical truth" and the discussion of *Nicomachean Ethics* Book VI, Chapter II on "choice." I will start from 1139a 21. "What affirmation and negation are in judgment, pursuit and avoidance are in desire." That is, one can say "yes" or "no" both to a statement and to a proposal. Suppose, then, that the statement should say that doing such and such is "doing well." There is the "yes" in judgment and the "yes" in the will, meaning that one wants to do that sort of thing. For to characterise it as "doing well" is *eo ipso* to propose it as an object of "will"—to put it up as a candidate for "will," *boulesis*.

"So," Aristotle goes on, "since moral virtue is a disposition of one's choice, while choice is deliberated wanting, these things show that the judgment must be true and the wanting right, if the choice is to be sound, and the one must say and the other pursue the same thing." We may remark that the one must say and the other pursue the same thing if there is to be any "choice" at all, sound or unsound. So far we have only mentioned the judgment on what *eupraxia*, doing well, is. A false judgment on this necessarily means that if there is a "choice" at all the wanting in it is wrong. To make this clear, imagine a worldling's idea of doing well. If the worldly man has any wants that are right, they don't occur in his "choices." Any "choice" that he makes, since in "choice" the wanting goes after what the judgment declares to be doing well, must involve wrong wanting.

Can the judgment be false at a lower level than one's idea of doing well, without the wanting being wrong if they are in accord? Suppose the man has judged truly, as Aristotle would say and as I want to say,

that to act justly is necessary for doing well, but falsely that justice would be done by dividing all the goods available in the country into equal shares according to the number of the population and assigning each share to one person by picking name and number of share out of a hat; or that it is justice for a poor man to be punished for assaulting a rich one, but not vice versa. I am not speaking of particular procedures, but of judgments about what *sort* of procedures are just.

It appears to me that only when we get to questions where it is difficult to know the truth, or questions as to facts which the agent can't be expected to have found out, is there any chance for the wanting of what is judged a means to doing well to be right when the judgment itself is wrong. This then will be why Aristotle said in Book III (1110b 31) that ignorance in choice, *he en te prohairesei agnoia*, is the cause not of involuntariness but of scoundrelism. He himself laid down the rule about difficulty at 1113b 33–1114a 2.

We now approach the great question: what does Aristotle mean by "practical truth"? He calls it the good working, or the work, of practical judgment; and practical judgment is judgment of the kind described, terminating in action. It is practical truth when the judgments involved in the formation of the "choice" leading to the action are all true; but the practical truth is not the truth of those *judgments*. For it is clearly that "truth in agreement with right desire," *aletheia homologos echousa te orexei te orthe* (1139a 30), which is spoken of as the good working (*eu*), or the work (*ergon*), of practical intelligence. That is brought about—i.e. made true—by action (since the description of what he does is made true by his doing it), provided that a man forms and executes a good "choice." The man who forms and executes an evil "choice" will also make true *some* description of what he does. He will secure, say, if he is competent, that such and such a man has his eyes put out or his hands cut off, that being his judgment of what it is just to do. But his description "justice performed" of what he has done will be a lie. He, then, will have produced practical falsehood.

"Since everything that is done about them is false, how should these be gods?"—The notion of *truth or falsehood in action* would quite generally be countered by the objection that "true" and "false" are senseless predicates as applied to what is done. If I am right there is philosophy to the contrary in Aristotle. And if, as I should maintain, the idea of the *description under which* what is done is done is integral to the notion of action, then these predicates apply to actions strictly and properly, and not merely by an extension and in a way that ought to be explained away.

ON FORGETTING THE
DIFFERENCE BETWEEN
RIGHT AND WRONG*

Gilbert Ryle

"Don't you know the difference between right and wrong?" *"Well, I did learn it once, but I have forgotten it."* This is a ridiculous thing to say. But why is it ridiculous? We forget lots of things, including lots of important things, that we used to know. So what is the absurdity in the idea of a person's forgetting the difference between right and wrong?

I think the question worthy of discussion, if only because the epistemological wheels on which ethical theories are made to run are apt to be wooden and uncircular.

Only one philosopher, so far as I know, has discussed my question. Aristotle does so very briefly in the *Nicomachean Ethics* 1100^b 17 and 1140^b 29.

First let us get rid of two possible misconstructions of my question.

In speaking of a person's knowing or not knowing the difference between right and wrong, I shall not be speaking of him as knowing or not knowing the solutions to philosophers' conceptual questions like, "What are the definitions of Rightness and Wrongness, respectively?" A properly brought up child knows the difference between right and wrong, for all that he has never heard an argument from Kant or Thrasymachus and would not have understood their definitions if he had. Anyhow, there is no absurdity in the idea of a philosophy student's having forgotten some ethical definitions or analyses that he had once known. He would not thereby cease to know the difference between right and wrong.

Next, the assertion that it is absurd to say that a person might forget the difference between right and wrong could be misconstrued

*Reprinted from A. I. Melden, ed., *Essays in Moral Philosophy* (Seattle, 1958), by permission of the author and the University of Washington Press.

as the ascription to our knowledge of right and wrong of an inspiring kind of indelibility, perhaps a Heaven-hinting innateness or a trailing cloud of glory. No such edifying moral can be looked for. If it is absurd to say that one has forgotten the difference, it is also absurd to say that one recollects it. If it is absurd to say that one's knowledge of the difference between right and wrong might, like one's Latin, get rusty, then it is also absurd to say that it actually remains, like one's English, unrusty.

1. It might be suggested that there is a quite simple reason why we cannot forget the difference between right and wrong, namely, that daily life gives us constant reminders of it. Somewhat as, throughout December, Christmas carols, Christmas cards, and butchers' shops constantly remind us of the imminence of Christmas Day, so the daily procession of duties to be done and derelictions to be apologized for keeps us constantly in mind of the difference between right and wrong. But this explanation will not do. A very forgetful person remains unreminded in the midst of reminders. Even the knot in his handkerchief does not remind him of anything. Moreover, a man might happen to sojourn in a part of the world where there were no reminders of Christmas. If this were all, then the maker of the paradoxical remark might just be in the rare position of being unusually forgetful or unusually unexposed to obligations; and then his remark would be not ridiculous but only hard to credit. Forgetting the difference between right and wrong would then be merely a rare thing, like forgetting one's own name.

This suggested explanation is a causal hypothesis. It offers to tell what makes people very unlikely to forget the difference between right and wrong. It therefore assumes that there is such a thing as forgetting this difference. But our question is, rather, "Why is there no such thing? Why will 'forget' and 'be reminded of' not go with 'the difference between right and wrong'?"

2. A better, though still inadequate, explanation would be this. Knowing the difference between right and wrong is of a piece not with remembering particular matters of fact, like names, dates, and engagements, but with knowing how to do things, knowing the way from place to place, knowing Latin, and knowing the rules of the road in one's own country. Such things do not slip our memories, nor are knots tied in our handkerchiefs to keep us in mind of them. Knowledge here is mastery of techniques rather than mere possession of information; it is a capacity that can improve or decline, but cannot just come in and go out. We acquire such knowledge not just from

being told things, but from being trained to do things. The knowledge is not imparted but inculcated. It is a second nature, and therefore not evanescent. Now our knowledge of the difference between right and wrong certainly is in many important respects much more like a mastery than like the retention of a piece of information. It is, for instance, inculcated by upbringing rather than imparted by dictation. It is not a set of things memorized and is not, consequently, the sort of knowledge of which shortness of memory is the natural enemy.

Nonetheless, there is such a thing as forgetting much or all of one's Latin. With desuetude, one does become rustier and rustier, until one has totally forgotten it. We know what we have to do to keep up our Latin, our geometry, or our tennis, namely, to give ourselves regular practice. Just here is one place where the analogy breaks down between knowing the difference between right and wrong and having mastery of a science or a craft. One's knowledge of the difference between right and wrong does not get rusty; we do not keep up our honesty by giving ourselves regular exercises in it. Nor do we excuse a malicious action by saying that we have recently been short of practice in fair-mindedness and generosity. Virtues are not proficiencies. The notion of being out of practice, which is appropriate to skills, is inappropriate to virtues.

Aristotle's explanation of the fact that there is no such thing as forgetting the difference between right and wrong seems to be that moral dispositions are, from constant exercise, much more abiding things than even our masteries of sciences and crafts. In the latter there is forgetting, though only gradual forgetting; in the former there happens to be none. But the difference does not seem to be just a difference in degree, or even just a difference between a small magnitude and zero. Nor is it just a matter of anthropological fact that our knowledge of the difference between right and wrong never decays. The notion of decay does not fit.

En passant, when I argue that we do not impose moral exercises upon ourselves in order to prevent our knowledge of the difference between right and wrong from rusting, since the notion of rusting does not belong, I am not denying that we can or should drill ourselves into good habits and out of bad ones. I am only denying that such self-disciplining is to be assimilated to the exercises by which we prevent our Latin or our tennis from getting rusty. The object of moral drills is not to save us from forgetting the difference between right and wrong, but to stiffen us against doing what we know to be wrong.

Neither, to make the obverse point, am I denying that moral

deterioration occurs. People often do get more callous, less public-spirited, meaner, lazier, and shiftier. What I am denying is that such deteriorations are to be assimilated to declines in expertness, i.e., to getting rusty.

√3. A third explanation would be this. Since virtues are not skills, that is, since to be unselfish or patient is not to be good *at* doing anything, perhaps virtues should be classed rather with tastes and preferences, and particularly with educated tastes and cultivated preferences. As the music lover had once to learn to appreciate music, and the bridge player had to learn both to play and to enjoy playing bridge, so the honest man had to be taught or trained to dislike deception, and the charitable man had to be taught or trained to want to relieve distress. Doubtless, as some people take to music from the start as a duck takes to water, so some people are naturally more prone than others to be frank and sympathetic. But to be honest or charitable on principle, even against the impulses of the moment, involves knowing the difference between right and wrong—much as, unlike the mere relishing of one piece of music more than another, appreciating the superiority of the one piece over the other involves knowing their relative merits and demerits. Taste is educated preference, preference for recognized superiorities. To be able to recognize superiorities is to know the difference between good and bad.

Now likings, whether natural or cultivated, can be lost. Most grown-ups have lost the enthusiasm for playing hide-and-seek, and some cease to enjoy tobacco and poetry. There can also be deteriorations in taste. A person who once had appreciated the excellences of Jane Austen might become so coarsened in palate as to cease to recognize or relish them.

It is relevant to my problem that we do not call such losses or deteriorations "forgetting." Perhaps the absurdity in speaking of someone's forgetting the difference between right and wrong is of a piece with the absurdity in speaking of someone who has lost the taste for poetry as having forgotten the difference between good and bad poetry.

When a person has an educated taste, he can speak of himself as having learned or been taught not only to recognize the differences between, say, good and bad singing or good and bad tennis strokes, but also to appreciate, i.e., to like, admire, and try for the good and to dislike, despise, and avoid the bad. Knowing, in this region, goes hand in hand with approving and disapproving, relishing and disrelishing, admiring and despising, pursuing and avoiding. Indeed, their connec-

tion seems even closer than mere hand-in-hand concomitance. There seems to be a sort of incongruity in the idea of a person's knowing the difference between good and bad wine or poetry, while not caring a whit more for the one than for the other; of his appreciating without being appreciative of excellences. When we read, "We needs must love the highest when we see it," we incline to say, "Of course. We should not be seeing it if we were not loving it. The 'needs must' is a conceptual one. At least in this field, the partitions are down between the Faculties of Cognition, Conation, and Feeling."

Now whether this inclination is justified or not, it exists just as much in our thinking about the knowledge of right and wrong. Here, too, there seems to be an incongruity in the idea of a person's knowing that something wrong had been done, but still not disapproving of it or being ashamed of it; of his knowing that something would be the wrong thing for him to do, but still not scrupling to do it. We hanker to say that, if he has no scruples at all in doing the thing, then he cannot know that it is wrong, but only, perhaps, that it is "wrong," i.e., what other people call "wrong."

Socrates used to ask the important question "Can Virtue be taught?" It puzzled him, very properly, that if virtue can be taught there exist no pundits in courage, abstinence, or justice. If we, too, think that knowledge of the difference between right and wrong is knowledge, ought we not to be puzzled that universities and technical colleges do not give courses in industriousness, fair-mindedness, and loyalty? But the moment such a suggestion is made, we realize that the non-existence of pundits and colleges of the virtues is not a lamentable lacuna in our society. It would be silly to try to provide such instruction; silly, since knowledge of the difference between right and wrong is not the sort of thing that such instruction could bestow. We continue to think that children have to be taught the difference between right and wrong, but we know in our bones that this teaching is not a species of either factual or technical instruction. What sort of teaching, then, is the teaching of the difference between right and wrong? What sort of learning is the learning of this difference? What kind of knowing is the knowing of it? Maybe we can approach an answer to these questions by considering the teaching and learning of tastes.

A person who has received technical instruction in tennis, music, or landscape gardening may, but may not, owe to his instructor a second debt of gratitude for having taught him also to enjoy these

things. A person who has learned from a geographer and a botanist the special features of the Lake District may have been inspired by Wordsworth also to love this district for these features. As one gets to know a person better, one may learn to respect or admire him. Learning to enjoy, to love, or to admire is not acquiring a skill or a parcel of information. Nonetheless it *is* learning. There is a difference between a mere change-over from disliking rice pudding to liking it, and learning to appreciate wines, poems, or people for their excellences. Learning to appreciate requires some studiousness, judiciousness, and acuteness. The judge has reasons to give for his likings, his verdicts, and his choices.

True, the special notions of *lessons, instruction, coaching, examinations, laboratories, courses, manuals,* and the like are no part of the idea of learning to enjoy or learning to admire. Even if Wordsworth really does teach us to love the Lake District, he does not merit or need a professor's chair. But this is only to say again that admiring, enjoying, and loving are not efficiencies or equipments. The notions of *learning, studying, teaching,* and *knowing* are ampler notions than our academic epistemologies have acknowleged. They are hospitable enough to house under their roofs notions like those of *inspiring, kindling,* and *infecting.*

It will be objected, I expect, that what is called "learning to enjoy" or "being taught to admire" is really always two processes, namely, (1) coming to know some things, and (2) as an effect of coming to know them, coming to like or admire. An emotional condition, disposition, or attitude is caused by a cognitive act or disposition. As the rolling of the ship makes me feel sick, so discovering a person's characteristics makes me experience feelings of admiration toward him. So, presumably, as certain nostrums save me from feeling sick when the ship rolls, certain other nostrums might save me from admiring a person when I have discovered what a stanch friend he is. Alternatively, if this sounds too ridiculous, then a peculiarly intimate kind of causal connection has to be invoked in order to represent the connection between knowing and admiring as still a causal one, and yet as one that is exempt from preventions.

If we ask what the supposedly antecedent process of coming to know consists in, we are likely to be told that it consists in coming to be equipped with some information or/and coming to be relatively efficient at doing certain sorts of things, *plus,* perhaps, coming to be able and ready to explain, instruct, criticize, and so forth. These are not effects of coming to know; they are concrete examples of what

coming to know is coming to. But why not add that sometimes coming to know *is*, also, *inter alia*, coming to admire or enjoy? If making a skillful tennis stroke or a skillful translation is doing something that one has learned to do, i.e., is an exercise and not an effect of knowledge, why may not admiring a person for his stanchness be, in a partly similar way, an example and not an aftereffect of what our study of his character has taught us? The reply that what is learned must be either a piece of information or a technique begs the question, since the question is, in part, "Why must it be either one or the other?"

How does all this apply to our knowledge of the difference between right and wrong? We are unwilling to allow that a person has learned this difference who does not, for instance, care a bit whether he breaks a promise or keeps it, and is quite indifferent whether someone else is cruel or kind. This *caring* is not a special feeling; it covers a variety of feelings, like those that go with being shocked, ashamed, indignant, admiring, emulous, disgusted, and enthusiastic; but it also covers a variety of actions, as well as readinesses and pronenesses to do things, like apologizing, recompensing, scolding, praising, persevering, praying, confessing, and making good resolutions. Now, if we consider what in detail a person who has learned the difference between right and wrong has learned, we do not naturally draw a line between some things, namely, what he has learned to say and do, and other things, namely, what he has learned to feel, and relegate the latter to the class of mere aftereffects of his learning to say and do the proper things. In thinking about his conscience or his sense of duty, we do not naturally fence off his qualms from his acts of reparation; his pangs from his confessings or his resolvings; his prickings from his perseverings. *Because* he has learned the difference between right and wrong, he both makes reparations and feels contrite; and the "because" is the same noncausal "because." Certainly his feeling contrite is not an exercise of a technique or the giving of a piece of information; but the same is true, though for different reasons, of his making reparations, persevering, reproaching, resolving, and keeping appointments. All are marks, though different sorts of marks, of his knowing the difference between right and wrong; all show, though in different ways, that he has principles, and what these principles are; any one of them is one of the many sorts of things that we have in mind when we say of him that he has a sense of duty.

Now we can begin to see why it is ridiculous to say that one has forgotten the difference between right and wrong. To have been taught the difference is to have been brought to appreciate the

difference, and this appreciation is not just a competence to label correctly or just a capacity to do things efficiently. It includes an inculcated caring, a habit of taking certain sorts of things seriously.

A person who used to care may, indeed, cease to care or to care so much. But ceasing to care is not forgetting, any more than ceasing to believe something or to mistrust someone is forgetting. "Forget" is reserved, apparently, mainly for the nonretention of information and the loss of skills through desuetude, though it is also used for ceasing to notice things, e.g., for the oblivion brought by sleep or distractions.

This use of "forget" for the loss of information and technical abilities, and its nonuse for cessations of caring, may go with another difference. If I have ceased to enjoy bridge, or come to admire Picasso, then *I* have changed. But, if I have forgotten a date or become rusty in my Latin, I do not think of this as a change in *me*, but rather as a diminution of my equipment. In the same way, a person who becomes less or more conscientious is a somewhat changed person, not a person with an enlarged or diminished stock of anything. In a testimonial both personal qualities and equipment need to be mentioned, but the equipment is not mentioned among the personal qualities.

So far I have been pressing some analogies between things like tastes and pastimes on the one hand and virtues on the other; I have concentrated on ways in which the notions of *learning, teaching,* and *knowing* lock in with notions of *caring,* i.e., *enjoying, admiring, despising, trying, avoiding,* and so forth; and I have tried to show how, in these connections, they detach themselves from the notion of *forgetting.* But we must not push assimilation to the point of identification.

The man who knows the difference between good and bad tennis strokes, and applauds or tries for the good ones and pities or avoids the bad ones, is something of a specialist. The man who appreciates wines is something of a connoisseur. They have acquired special technical abilities and, therewith, special enjoyments. We others may envy them for both. But knowledge of the difference between right and wrong is common knowledge, and it is not mastery of a technique. There is nothing in particular that the honest man knows, ex officio, how to do. He is not, ex officio, even a bit of an expert at anything. Nor is his life enriched by some extra relishes. He possesses nothing for us to envy.

Often, though not always, we study to become relatively good at things, e.g., games, fine arts, and recreations, because we either enjoy them from the start or anyhow expect to get pleasure from them in the end. Our elders coerce us into learning to swim, largely because they

think that we shall miss a lot of pleasure afterward if we do not learn to swim, or to swim well. But this is nothing like the reason or reasons for which elders train the young to be honest. The truth lover has no treats to match against those of the music lover. A sense of duty is not an esthetic sensibility; nor is the passion for righteousness indulged as the passion for bridge or birdwatching is indulged. It is not addiction to a sport or hobby. Certainly there are activities, like most work, in which, although technical excellence pleases and bad craftsmanship displeases, still the jobs are not done or even done well only for pleasure's sake. But the honest or charitable man has not, ex officio, any particular job to do, much less to be proud of doing well rather than botching. Knowing the difference between right and wrong is not identical with knowing the difference between good and bad work, even though they resemble one another in the fact that ceasing to care how one does one's job, like ceasing to care what one does, is not a case of forgetting.

One more reinsurance. I have claimed to detect an incongruity, and the same sort of incongruity, in the idea of a man's knowing the difference between right and wrong but not caring a bit whether he lies, say, or tells the truth; in the idea of a man's recognizing, without being appreciative of, the excellences of Jane Austen; and in the idea of a craftsman's knowing the difference between good and bad workmanship without taking any pride in his own good work or feeling any contempt for the bad work of others. I may seem to have equated this knowing with having learned to take seriously. But there is a trap here.

I may be a bit shocked and indignant at an exhibition of unfairness, while you are much shocked and highly indignant. I care a bit about it, and you care much more. But this does not involve that you know more differences between right and wrong than I do, if this makes any sense, or that you know the difference better, if this makes any sense. Similarly, a specimen of Shakespeare's literary genius may please me while it thrills you. We appreciate the same excellence, though we are unequally appreciative of it. So even if, in some domains, to teach is, *inter alia*, to kindle, still we do not think of what is taught as varying in magnitude with the heat of the fire. The match is the same, but the fuels are different.

One last point. In most fields instructors can misinstruct. I may be taught that the Battle of Hastings was fought in 1077, and I may be taught to grip fiercely my billiard cue and my steering wheel. While I retain faith in my instructor, I shall still claim to know the date of the

battle and to know how to control the cue and the steering wheel; but when I have learned better, I shall agree that I had not formerly known the date of the battle or how to control the cue or the wheel. I have to unlearn what I was originally taught.

There is no difficulty in conceiving of misinstruction in the particular articles of codes of etiquette. A boy might well be trained to remain respectfully hatted in a lady's drawing room and punctiliously to end his letters to tradesmen with "Yours sincerely." Nor is there much difficulty in conceiving of misinstruction in some of the bylaws of morality. Some people used scrupulously to pay all their gambling debts before paying off any of their debts to servants and tradesmen. Their consciences had been educated to insist on this priority.

But there is a difficulty in conceiving of a person's being taught to be selfish, deceitful, cruel, and lazy on principle; to be morally shocked at exhibitions of fair-mindedness; or scrupulously to make reparations for his backslidings into unselfishness. The notion of moral non-education is familiar enough, but the notion of moral miseducation has a smell of absurdity. There is a whiff of the same smell of absurdity in the notion of the would-be connoisseur of wines or engravings being mistaught, taught, that is, to relish wines for their immaturity or to admire engravings for their smudginesses. However, the smell of absurdity is less strong here. The Albert Memorial does seem to have been admired for its architectural badnesses.

The oddness, if it exists, in the idea of moral miseducation might be one source of the strength of the notion of The Moral Law. But to follow up this train of thought would seduce me into talking Ethics.

ARISTOTLE AND THE PUNISHMENT OF PSYCHOPATHS*

Vinit Haksar

In a paper called "The Responsibility of Psychopaths,"[1] I think I succeeded in establishing that we cannot rule out *a priori* the possibility that psychopaths may be shown to be lacking in responsibility. I also examined some arguments that try to show the psychopath to be lacking in responsibility, but I concluded that these arguments were not very successful. In this paper I intend to make and examine some more attempts at showing the psychopath to be lacking in responsibility. But before I do that there is one point to keep in mind.

There is one theory according to which no one is responsible. (Some of those who believe in this theory do so because they believe that determinism is true and because they believe that determinism is incompatible with responsibility.) If this theory is correct, then *a fortiori*, psychopaths are not responsible. But this theory is inconsistent with our present system of criminal and moral responsibility; if we accept this theory then we shall have to get rid of our system of responsibility—for our system of responsibility assumes that some people are responsible, while some are not.

So the point we should keep in mind is this: As long as we operate within our system of responsibility, any argument that tries to excuse psychopaths will, other things being equal, be much more convincing if it shows why we should excuse psychopaths *while* we continue to punish many other criminals.

I

It has been said that though in a sense (let us call it the narrower sense) psychopaths know that their behaviour is wrong, i.e. they know

* Reprinted from *Philosophy*, Oct. 1964, by permission of the author and The Royal Institute of Philosophy. I wish to thank Prof. H. L. A. Hart and Prof. W. C. Kneale for valuable suggestions.
[1] *Philosophical Quarterly*, 1965.

that their activities are against the law and against the moral code of the society they are living in, yet in another sense (let us call it the wider sense) they do not know that it is wrong, they are lacking in a conscience, are morally and emotionally hollow and are incapable of really appreciating the nature of what they are doing. As a result of such ignorance, they do not conform to the law, and are incapable of wanting to conform to the law.[2]

Against this it might be pointed out that though this (i.e. the wider sense) may be a perfectly legitimate sense of knowing, it is not the sense which is relevant for excusing a person from blame or punishment. Aristotle and others have argued that every wicked man is ignorant of what he ought to do and what he ought to abstain from, and that such ignorance does not excuse. But what if the agent is not responsible for such ignorance—e.g., suppose he is ignorant because he had a bad education and upbringing? Here it might be said that the problem is not whether the psychopath is incapable of becoming moral, but whether he is incapable of conforming to the law. This point of course does not solve the problem, but only tells us that the problem we have to face needs to be distinguished from another problem. The problem that we shall have to face is this: Even if the psychopath does not have to become moral in order to become law-abiding, in view of the fact of his education, upbringing, etc., is it fair to punish him or to blame him for not conforming to the law? Here two tests seem relevant.

1. How far could he have avoided acquiring criminal values? Even if a man cannot get rid of his criminal values, once he has

---

[2] Cf. "Ley, because of his insanity, lived in a twilight world of distorted values which resulted not so much in his being 'incapable of preventing himself' from committing his crime, in the strict sense of those words, as in his being incapable of appreciating, as a sane man would, why he should try to prevent himself from committing it. It seems to us reasonable to argue that the words 'incapable of preventing himself' should be construed so as to cover such states of mind; that they should be interpreted as meaning not merely that the accused was incapable of preventing himself if he had tried to do so, but that he was incapable of wishing or of trying to prevent himself, or incapable of realising or attending to considerations which might have prevented him if he had been capable of attending to them. If each of Ley's acts is considered separately, it would be difficult to maintain that he could not have prevented himself from committing them. Yet if his course of conduct is looked at as a whole, it might well be argued that he was incapable of preventing himself from conceiving the murderous scheme, incapable of judging it by other than an insane scale of ethical values, and in that sense, incapable of preventing himself from carrying it out." *Royal Commission on Capital Punishment.* Cmd. 8932. page 111.

acquired them, he may have been able to avoid acquiring them in the past.

2. Once he acquired criminal values, how far could he have got rid of them? Even if his criminal values were originally the result of causes outside his control, a man may still be able to get rid of these values.

Now if we judge by these two tests, why is the psychopath any less responsible than most other criminals who have criminal values?

The concept of psychopathy had not been invented in Aristotle's time, but Aristotle[3] says things which commit him to saying that psychopaths do pass the first test. I think Aristotle's arguments on this point are not wholly convincing. Aristotle argues that men become unjust and self-indulgent by doing activities in the past which, unless they were thoroughly senseless, they must have known would make them develop an unjust and self-indulgent character. Therefore, they are responsible for acquiring their characters.

One could make more than one criticism of this argument of Aristotle's. Firstly, it may be said that many wicked men (and not only those among them who were thoroughly senseless) though in a sense (i.e., in the narrower sense) they knew in the past that their actions will make them develop a wicked character, yet in another sense (i.e., the wider sense) they did not really know this. Children, for instance, do not know all that is involved in being wicked, for they are morally and emotionally not developed. So Aristotle's argument is either redundant or it is not wholly convincing. For if all that is required for responsibility is knowledge in the narrower sense, then men, even after they have acquired a wicked character, have this knowledge and so we need not try to show that they were responsible for becoming wicked. But if knowledge in the narrower sense is not enough for responsibility, then Aristotle's argument is not wholly persuasive. For at least in many cases unjust and self-indulgent men in the past may only have had knowledge in the narrower sense.

And there is another criticism that can be made of Aristotle's argument. For this argument of Aristotle's assumes that knowledge is a sufficient condition of responsibility.[4] But this assumption can be criticised. For even if a man knew (both in the narrower and in the wider sense) in the past that by indulging in certain activities he would develop the corresponding character, he may not have had a fair

---

[3] See *The Nicomachean Ethics* of Aristotle, Book III, Section 5.

[4] Aristotle does not always assume this. Thus he allows duress as an excuse.

choice. Nature might have been unkind to him in a way that made it difficult for him to exercise self-control. Or even if nature had been kind, the pressure of circumstances might have been very great. Even if one can always try, within the limits set by nature and circumstances, is it not more difficult for him (i.e. the man to whom nature or circumstances have been cruel) to conform to the law, than it is for those who have been more generously treated?

Many of us do believe that other things being equal, the more unkind nature and circumstances have been to a person, the more compassionate we should be in judging that person.

And, *a fortiori*, we believe that, other things being equal, the more unkind nature and circumstances have been to a criminal the more compassionate we should be in judging that criminal.

This principle is, I think, a good one, and is relevant to the first test (page 81). For whether the criminal had a fair choice in the past of avoiding criminal values, does depend upon the way that nature and circumstances have treated him.

Now in order to apply this principle two conditions must be satisfied.

1. We should be able to say, at least roughly, what conditions must be satisfied before we are justified in saying that nature or environment has been kind or unkind to a person. This is not an easy problem. For sometimes nature or circumstances may appear harsh when in fact they are giving blessings in disguise. And sometimes nature and environment are really harsh when the opposite appears to be the case. Take, for example, criminals who come from wealthy and "happy" families. We may be tempted to say that they are more blameworthy than those who come from poor families. Yet the criminal who comes from the wealthy and "happy" family may have had his own problems—e.g., he may have been, through no fault of his, spoilt at home as a child, and as a result it might have become difficult for him to stand up in this world and "face reality." Lovers of equality, like Rousseau, have been at pains to show that inequalities harm both the poor and the rich.

2. Even if we know what conditions are favourable and what conditions are unfavourable, there is the problem of getting enough evidence about a man's life history to be able to say whether he satisfies the relevant conditions. This is a formidable problem even with people whom we know well; it becomes much more so in the Law Courts, where the criminal is not well known to those who have to decide what is to be done with him.

It is perhaps because of these two difficulties that our legal system does not *always* go into the question of how far the criminal could have acted otherwise in the past. Thus if a criminal falls under the *McNaughton Rules* or the *Homicide Act*, then we do excuse him, though neither the *McNaughton Rules* nor the *Homicide Act* goes into the question of how far the criminal was responsible for acquiring the mental disorder.[5] It is true that in applying the *Homicide Act* and the *McNaughton Rules* we do often go into the agent's past (i.e., prior to his committing the crime), but we do this not with a view to finding out how far he could have helped things in the past, how far he was negligent in acquiring his disorder, but with a view to finding out about his mental condition and capacity to choose at the time he did the crime.

In view of all this how do psychopaths fare under the first test (i.e., the first test on page 81)? Because of the difficulties of applying this test, it is not easy to say that psychopaths come off worse than ordinary criminals. Perhaps, many psychopaths do come off worse than many "ordinary" criminals, but some ordinary criminals may come off worse than some psychopaths. It is not at all obvious that it is because a man is a psychopath that he comes off worse under the first test.

So what follows is that where the difficulties of applying this test are not great, this test should be applied. But this does not show that we ought to excuse a man *because* he is a psychopath.

Aristotle did not attach importance to the second test, because he believed that all except the thoroughly senseless pass the first test.[6] But we have seen that Aristotle was wrong in thinking that the first test is easy to apply and in thinking that only the thoroughly senseless people fail this test; and since Aristotle was wrong on these points, the second test becomes more important than it otherwise would have been. So let

[5] It is worth contrasting this with Aristotle's position. Aristotle says "wickedness is like a disease" (*ibid.*, Bk. VII, Section 8). This may seem inconsistent with his view that the wicked ought to be punished and blamed. But this apparent inconsistency would not have worried Aristotle. For he believed that all except the thoroughly senseless are responsible for becoming wicked. Similarly with drunkenness, Aristotle says it is no excuse whenever we are responsible for becoming drunk.

[6] When I say that a man passes the first test, I mean he could have avoided acquiring criminal values. When I say a man fails the first test I mean he could not have avoided acquiring criminal values. Similarly, by passing the second test, I mean the man could get rid of his criminal values, and by failing it, I mean he could not get rid of his criminal values. If A fails the test, and B passes the test, then A comes off worse under that test.

us now see whether the psychopath comes off any worse under the second test than most other criminals.

It might be suggested that the psychopath is more different from the ordinary law-abiding citizen than the ordinary criminal is. Both the ordinary criminal and the psychopath, unlike the ordinary law-abiding citizen, have criminal values. But the way of life of the ordinary criminal is more like the way of life of the ordinary law-abiding citizen than the way of life of the psychopath is. And so it is more difficult for the psychopath to change his condition and become like the law-abiding citizen than it is for the ordinary criminal. And so the psychopath is less responsible for committing crimes than the ordinary criminal is.

This chain of reasoning, it may be objected, contains at least one fallacy.

(a) Adopt the ways of life of the ordinary law-abiding citizen.

(b) Become law abiding.

It may be that the psychopath will find it more difficult to answer demand (a) than the ordinary criminal will. But it does not follow that the psychopath will find it more difficult to answer demand (b) than the ordinary criminal will. Now in deciding whether someone should be excused from punishment it is demand (b) that is relevant. The psychopath is not being asked to give up all his "peculiar" habits but only those which bring him into conflict with the law. Can a man in our society not lead a fairly chaotic and psychopath-like life without committing a crime?

Of course, the psychopath will find it quite difficult to get rid of his criminal values, but as yet we have not shown that he will find this substantially more difficult than the ordinary criminal will find the getting rid of his criminal wants.

But is it not easier in our society for the ordinary criminal[7] to

---

[7] "The (ordinary) criminal, in short, is usually trying to get something we all want, though he uses methods we shun. On the other hand the psychopath, if he steals or defrauds seems to do so for a much more obscure purpose." (H. Cleckley, *The Mask of Sanity*, 3rd edition, p. 292.)

In this paper, for reasons of space, I shall not say much about the characteristics of psychopaths. I have said something about this in "The Responsibility of Psychopaths." Those who wish to know more about what a psychopath is could read *The Mask of Sanity* by Cleckley.

In this paper I have assumed that, though psychopaths may be capable of good theoretical reasoning in moral and intellectual matters, they are lacking in moral sentiments (i.e., they do not have moral principles, they do not feel morally guilty when they do wrong, etc.). And I have also assumed that psychopaths

fulfil his needs without committing crimes? For our society offers more non-criminal channels for the satisfaction of conventional needs than for the satisfaction of the unconventional needs that psychopaths have. Perhaps a society could be constructed where the psychopath will find it as easy, or even easier, to satisfy his needs than the "ordinary" criminal will, but this does not alter the fact that in our society the psychopath finds it more difficult to satisfy his needs without committing a crime. And this makes it more difficult for the psychopath to give up his criminal ways. And so the psychopath is less responsible.

In assessing this argument three points are worth making. Firstly, an ordinary criminal may originally commit a crime out of a conventional motive (e.g., desire for money), but may after some time become addicted to the criminal way of life. He may then find it as difficult to give up his criminal values as a psychopath does. We can describe this situation by saying that the man was an ordinary criminal but after some time he ceased to be an ordinary criminal. And the fact that, once a man has ceased to be an ordinary criminal and has become addicted to crime, he finds it as difficult to give up his way of life as the psychopath does, is quite consistent with the view that while he was an ordinary criminal, it was easier for him to change his criminal ways than it was for the psychopath. The second point worth noticing is this. The reason why the ordinary criminal is likely to find it easier to give up his criminal ways is that since he has conventional needs (e.g., making money) these needs could be satisfied in ways other than committing a crime. But this is not always so. Sometimes a man may find that his need (e.g., need for food) is a conventional one, but circumstances are such that he has no way of satisfying his need except by committing a crime (e.g., if he is very poor, cannot get a job, if the State makes no provision for the poor, etc.), then for such a man it may be as difficult to give up his ways as it is for the psychopath. (Such a man, it would seem, should be excused, along with the psychopath.) But there will be other ordinary criminals who commit a

---

persistently commit anti-social actions and are more different from the average citizen than the ordinary criminal is.

In "The Responsibility of Psychopaths" I said that once we realise that psychopaths have different aims and values, *some* of the arguments that try to show the psychopath to be lacking in responsibility will be seen to break down. It would, however, be quite consistent to go on and try to show that psychopaths are not responsible with the help of the fact that their aims and values are very different.

crime because of conventional needs which they could satisfy in non-criminal ways (e.g., a man has quite a lot of money, but wants some more. He does not want to take the trouble of earning it, so he takes the easy way out and steals some money). Such criminals will find it easier to change their ways than the psychopath will. So it seems that strictly speaking we should say that psychopaths, like some ordinary criminals, but unlike some other ordinary criminals, will fail the second test. Of course, a lot will depend upon how we define "ordinary criminals." We could define "ordinary criminals" in such a way that those who commit a crime to satisfy conventional needs, but who are compelled to resort to criminal ways (e.g., because of economic necessity), are not "ordinary criminals." In this way we would still be able to say that the psychopath, unlike the ordinary criminal, fails the second test. But if under "ordinary criminals" we include all those who commit a crime to satisfy a conventional need, then we will have to say what we said a little earlier, i.e., psychopaths, like some ordinary criminals, but unlike some other ordinary criminals, fail the second test. And the third point worth observing is this. It is true that not all unconventional needs are difficult to satisfy in our society without breaking the law. Thus if, on getting up every morning, you need to go round and round your bed, this is an unconventional need but it can be easily satisfied without breaking the law. With psychopaths, how-ever, one gets the impression that their unconventional needs are not so innocent; much of their satisfaction, their cheap thrills, seem to consist in being reckless and in committing the crime. It may be true that they are not *completely* reckless but they are much more reckless than, say, the ordinary criminal or the pleasure-loving hedonist who adheres to the law. And with psychopaths their committing the crime is not just a means to some further end that could be reached in other ways; rather their criminal and anti-social behaviour is, if not the whole, at least a large part of the end they are seeking. But cannot they stop seeking this end? Even if their need is an unconventional one and cannot be satisfied in non-criminal ways, how do we know that their need is a strong one? It may be answered that they have been spending much of their life seeking these ends, and so have become quite addicted to them.[8]

---

[8] Aristotle says things which commit him to saying that psychopaths fail the second test. He says about the self-indulgent and unjust men "Now that they have become so it is not possible for them not to be so" (*ibid.*, Book III, Section 5).

At this point those who do not wish to excuse the psychopath may make a radical objection. They may concede that psychopaths do fail the second test, but they may go on to argue that this test is not a good method of showing lack of responsibility. For according to this test, many political criminals, such as Gandhi and Russell and their followers, will also be found lacking in responsibility. Even if it is true that psycopaths are lacking in a conscience and are morally and emotionally hollow, is it any easier for those who are morally and emotionally stuffed with values that are basically antithetical to those prevailing in the society, to conform to the law? So even if it is true that there is a sense of "can" in which psychopaths cannot conform to the law, it seems that in this sense political criminals also cannot conform to the law. So how could this be the sense of "can" which is relevant for excuses? It is probably true that political criminals can conform to the law in another sense of "can," i.e., in the sense that if they choose to conform to the law, then they will succeed in conforming to the law. But in *this* sense of "can" it has not been shown that psychopaths cannot conform to the law.

So why should psychopaths not be regarded as responsible, while political criminals are regarded as responsible?

Those wishing to excuse the psychopath may try to reply something like this: True, the sense of "can" in which the political criminals and psychopaths cannot conform to the law is not sufficient for distinguishing the responsible from those lacking in responsibility, but this sense of "can" can still be relevant for distinguishing the responsible from those lacking in responsibility. Both the political criminal and the psychopath fail the second test. But there is a difference. For political criminals are mentally healthy, while psychopaths are sick. And so psychopaths should be excused but political criminals should not.

This reasoning assumes that failure of the second test does not always diminish responsibility. It does so when another condition is also satisfied, namely that the agent is sick.

But what then is the use of the second test? Is it not redundant? Since both the sick and the healthy can fail this test, therefore we must have some independent way of distinguishing the sick and the healthy. And if we have this independent method of distinguishing the sick from the healthy, then why cannot we excuse the sick criminal and punish the healthy criminal without appealing to the second test?

Those wishing to defend the second test have a good answer to this question. They can say that though from the fact that a man has

failed the second test we cannot infer that he should be excused, and though we do need an independent method of distinguishing the sick from the healthy, yet this second test is not redundant. For not all mentally sick people are excused, but only a sub-class of them is excused.[9] If a man is mentally sick, this is not sufficient to excuse him, but if a man is both (a) mentally sick *and* as a result of this he (b) fails the second test, then this is jointly sufficient to show that he ought to be excused.[10]

Now if what has been said in the last paragraph is true, and I think it at least seems true, then: if psychopaths fail the second test, and if this happens because they are sick, then it follows that they ought to be excused. We have heard a good case for the view that psychopaths fail the second test. But we have not yet shown that psychopaths are sick. So we have yet to show that psychopaths should be excused.

In the next section I shall make another attempt at showing that psychopaths are sick.

II

In the paper called "The Responsibility of Psychopaths" I discussed the argument that psychopaths are sick because their behaviour is destructive of their aims and values. I think I succeeded in showing that once we realise that their aims and values may be different from ours, it is not at all obvious that their behaviour is destructive of their aims and values.

But even if we do not show that a man is pursuing means that are destructive of his ends, we might infer that he is mad if he chooses certain ends. This argument is sometimes used by those who are

---

[9] That something like this view is adhered to under our present system can be seen by examining the *McNaughton Rules* and *Homicide Act*. Under the *McNaughton Rules*, not all those who suffer from defect of reason due to disease of the mind are excused; only a sub-class of them is excused. The defect of reason must be of such a kind as to show that either (a) the accused did not know the nature or quality of his act or (b) if he did know this, he did not know that it was wrong.

Similarly, under the *Homicide Act*, it is not enough to show that the accused was suffering from abnormality of mind. Only a sub-class of the mentally abnormal is excused. For the abnormality of mind must be such that it "substantially impaired his mental responsibility for his acts and omissions in doing or being party to the killing." (*Homicide Act* 1957 Section 2.)

[10] Ideally, this point needs qualification. Even if a man satisfies these two conditions, we might feel, as Aristotle would have felt, that he ought not to be excused, if he was responsible for acquiring his illness. But we saw earlier that neither the *McNaughton Rules* nor the *Homicide Act* worries about this.

objectivists with regard to values, i.e., those who think that values are part of the universe, are discovered by human beings, and are not just human creations. An example of an objectivist who uses this argument is Sir Isaiah Berlin. He says ". . . if I say of someone that he is kind or cruel, loves truth or is indifferent to it, he remains human in either case. But if I find a man to whom it literally makes no difference whether he kicks a pebble or kills his family, since either would be an antidote to *ennui* or inactivity, I shall not be disposed, like consistent relativists, to attribute to him merely a different code of morality from my own or that of most men, or declare that we disagree on essentials, but shall begin to speak of insanity and inhumanity: I shall be inclined to consider him mad, as a man who thinks he is Napoleon is mad. . . . It is considerations such as these, urged by neo-Aristoteleans and the followers of the later doctrine of Wittgenstein, that have shaken the faith of some devoted empiricists in the complete logical gulf between descriptive statements and statements of value, and have cast doubt on the celebrated distinction derived from Hume."[11] Now this argument can be divided into two parts.

(a) The values that a man has are sometimes good evidence for the view that the man is mentally disordered.

(b) For (a) to be true, it is necessary that values should be objective. Since (a) is true, therefore the celebrated distinction that Hume drew between facts and values breaks down.

Now I think (a) may well be true, but (b) seems true because of a confusion. To clear the confusion, we should distinguish between two senses in which values could be said to exist.

(1) Values exist in the sense that men do as a matter of fact have values. We can make true statements about the values that people have. For instance, it is as a matter of fact true to say that the scale of values of a liberal are different from the scale of values of a Nazi.

(2) Values are real and objective in the sense that there are values in nature. Values are not mere human inventions imposed by man on a valueless reality; they belong to reality and man's job is to discover them.

Both those who are subjectivists with regard to the nature of values (e.g., Hume, Sartre, Ayer, Stevenson) and those who are objectivists (e.g., Plato, Aristotle, Prichard, Mrs P. Foot) on this issue

11 *Philosophy, Politics and Society.* Second Series. Edited by Laslett. Page 27.

would agree that values exist in sense one. It is only on the problem about whether values exist in sense two that the subjectivist and the objectivist part company.

Now if we are going to use the values that a man pursues as evidence of his insanity, then values must exist in sense one; but it is not at all obvious that values must exist in sense two.

Once we realise that there is an important sense in which creations exist, we cannot rule out the possibility that even if values are not objective in sense two, we may be able to use the fact that a man has created certain values as evidence about his mental condition. Just as there is nothing absurd in trying to understand about a man's mental condition from the paintings that he has created.

Of course, we have not solved all the problems. Suppose someone says that the values that a psychopath pursues are good evidence of mental disorder, while someone else says: No, they are not. How do we decide who is right?

This is an important difficulty, but this is a difficulty that I think has to be faced both by the subjectivists and by the objectivists. An objectivist may argue that values must exist in sense two if we are going to talk of moral insanity or dissociation from values. Against this, two considerations could be pointed out. First, moral insanity or dissociation from values is not the only kind of insanity that is relevant to excusing a person. There are other species of mental disorder that can exist (e.g., schizophrenia, psychosis, kleptomania) even if values do not exist in sense two. And it is not absurd to use the values that a man is pursuing as evidence of his mental disorder, even if values do not exist in sense two, and even if the disorder does not consist of moral insanity or dissociation from values. Secondly, it could be pointed out that even if values do not exist in sense two, we *can* still have moral insanity or dissociation from values. Even if values are not objective in sense two, a man may, due to mental disorder, be unable to choose certain ends. He can then be said to be dissociated from these ends.

Of course, there are difficulties here. E.g., how do we distinguish the mentally disordered from the mentally healthy? But such difficulties will have to be faced even if values are objective in sense two. For suppose values are objective in sense two. Then, of those who do not discover the truth in moral matters, how do we distinguish the dissociated from the rest, e.g., from those who are ignorant in some important moral matters because of their negligence or from those who are sane and yet can not reasonably be expected to know any

better? It may be that one need not distinguish the dissociated from those who are sane and yet cannot reasonably be expected to know any better, for the difference may not be an important one from the point of view of excusing people from blame or punishment. But we would still need to distinguish the dissociated from those who are sane and are ignorant in moral matters because of their negligence, for ignorance is no excuse where we could reasonably have avoided being ignorant, and this would be as true of ignorance of moral facts as it is of non-moral facts.

And there is another problem that the objectivist will have to face. Of those who have seen the truth in moral matters, but chosen not to adopt the ends that they have discovered, how do we distinguish those who have done this because they are mentally disordered from those who have done this in spite of being healthy (this distinction does seem important for the problem of excuses), e.g., suppose a psychopath discovers that crimes should not be committed, but goes on to choose a criminal way of life, how do we decide whether he is disordered or not? As long as we allow that there are people who see certain ends, yet try to regulate their lives not by the ends they have discovered but by different ones, can we rule out that many healthy people may belong to this class of people?[12] Objectivists may adhere to the dogma that those who do not have a strong propensity for doing what they have discovered to be the case in moral matters, must be sick. Or, alternatively, the objectivists may try to show that the class of people who see certain ends, yet try to regulate their lives not by the ends they have discovered, but by different ones, is a null class. They may try to show this by adopting some such metaphysical dogma as this.[13] Human beings have a strong propensity for doing what they have discovered to be the case in moral matters; or, unless one has a strong

---

[12] This class of people is, of course, not identical with the class of those who want to regulate their lives by certain ends, yet find they are unable to do so, e.g., because of irresistible impulses.

[13] Of course, some objectivists may not believe in any such dogma. They may take the view that those who choose to regulate their lives by ends that are different from the ends that they have discovered, can be presumed to be healthy unless they can be shown to be sick in some other way, e.g., if a man believes he is the king of France, and if he is indifferent between kicking a pebble and the destruction of his family, we may infer that he is mad, not from the fact that he is indifferent between kicking the pebble and the destruction of his family, but from the fact that he believes he is the king of France.

But, of course, those like Berlin, who wish to use the scale of values that a man has as evidence of his madness, cannot take this position.

propensity for doing an action, one cannot discover that one has an obligation to do it.[14] By calling this sort of view a dogma, I do not necessarily mean that it is false; but that it needs to be supported by argument and empirical evidence. Even if such support is forthcoming, not *all* problems will be solved for the objectivist. For instance the problem we mentioned a little earlier, about how to distinguish those who are ignorant in moral matters because they are dissociated, from those who are ignorant in moral matters because of negligence, will still need to be solved.

Of course, this method of using a man's values as evidence of his sickness *can* be used not just in establishing moral sickness, but in establishing non-moral sicknesses also. But both the objectivist and the

---

[14] Aristotle seems to have held some such metaphysical view. It is significant that he believes that wrong doers must either be ignorant of the universal (he says "all wicked men are ignorant of what they ought to do, and what they ought to abstain from"), or do something against choice (he says "incontinence is contrary to choice"). He, implicitly, denies the existence of people who choose to regulate their lives by principles that they know to be wrong. And in our own day the theory of the integration of the self has been used (e.g., by Jerome Hall. See his *General Principles of Criminal Law*, 2nd edition, Chapter 13) to rule out, explicitly or implicitly, the following classes of people: (a) those who know the right ends, but choose to regulate their lives by ends that are radically different, and (b) those who know what is right and good and wish to do what is right and good, but do wrong because their power of self-control is diseased. They rule out the above classes of people on the grounds that the important powers of the personality (e.g., knowledge, volition, emotion) are integrated, and so one important power cannot be impaired, unless all the other important powers are also impaired. ("Serious mental disease is an impairment of all the principal aspects of the personality" (Jerome Hall: *General Principles of Criminal Law*, 2nd edition, page 494).) To deny this would entail, so the argument runs, the acceptance of the out-dated faculty psychology, according to which the mind was divided into separate compartments. For if the mind is not divided into separate compartments, a disease that has impaired one important power must have impaired the other important powers also.

It seems to me, however, that one can accept the view that one important power of the mind (e.g., volition) can be diseased while another important power (e.g., knowledge) is unimpaired, without believing in any of the errors of faculty psychology. One can, for instance, agree with Ellis ". . . a person's ego, id or superego cannot do, under its own power, anything whatever. It is in the case of any normal adult human being, the whole person, or individual or organism who thinks, emotes and acts." (Quoted by Hall, page 597.) Yet even if the mind is not divided into separate compartments, even if what Ellis says in the above quotation is correct, it is still possible that some of a person's powers may be seriously impaired while others are not. It is perhaps true that if the mind is not divided into separate compartments *and if* the disease is contagious between different powers of the mind, then one important power cannot be seriously diseased without impairing the other important powers. But why must the disease *always* be contagious between different powers of the mind?

subjectivist will have the problem of distinguishing the sick from the healthy, e.g., is the fact that a man is indifferent between kicking a pebble and the destruction of his family good evidence that he is psychotic? Or neurotic?

What then are we to make of this method of distinguishing the disordered from the healthy by a study of the ends that people are pursuing?

Berlin may be right in his belief that values exist in sense two, but I have tried to show that Berlin is wrong in implying that this method of showing insanity can only be used if values exist in sense two.[15] I have tried to show that, whether or not values exist in sense two, it is not absurd to use this method. Hume says "It is not contrary to reason to prefer the destruction of the whole world to the scratching of my finger. It is not contrary to reason for me to choose my total ruin, to prevent the least uneasiness of an Indian, or person wholly unknown to me." This is an illustration of Hume's view that values do not exist in sense two. But it would seem quite *consistent* for Hume to go on to say that the man who prefers the destruction of the whole world to the scratching of his finger is irrational in the sense that he is insane, even morally insane. This point may need a little qualification. Sometimes a distinction is drawn between mental sickness and insanity. Insanity entails sickness; but the converse is not true. Insanity involves cognitive disorders (e.g., psychosis) as a result of which the patient's vision of facts is impaired—he loses touch with reality. But there are other kinds of mental sicknesses, which involve only volitional disorder, and here the patient may see facts properly, but is unable to control himself (e.g., neurosis).

Similarly one can coin a distinction (as far as I know no one takes the trouble of making this distinction) between moral insanity and moral sickness. Moral insanity would entail moral sickness but the converse would not hold. Moral insanity would involve inability to see moral facts. But there would be other kinds of moral sicknesses which involve not inability to see moral facts, but inability to choose certain values. This inability to choose certain values may itself be a result of (mental) insanity or of some other kind of mental sickness.

---

[15] I think Berlin, in his valuable and exciting paper, has made this mistake. For he does imply, in the passage that I quoted earlier, that consistent relativists will say that the man who has very different values from us is not mad. But if there is anything of value to be learnt from a discussion of this mistake, it should remain, even if I am wrong in attributing this mistake to Berlin.

We thus have:

1. Mental sicknesses
   (a) Insanity
   (b) Other kinds of mental sicknesses.

2. Moral sicknesses
   (a) Moral insanity
   (b) Other kinds of moral sicknesses.

There is nothing logically absurd in using the ends that a man is pursuing as evidence of any of the above kinds of sicknesses.

Only 2(a) is incompatible with the thesis of subjectivists like Hume. And it is worth observing that it is only in this sense that moral insanity is incompatible with Hume's position. If we use moral insanity in another sense, in which it is synonymous with moral sickness, then it is not incompatible with Hume's views. Corresponding to the two senses of moral insanity, we can have two senses of "dissociation from values." In one sense it means inability, due to mental disorder, to see values properly. In the second sense, it means inability, due to mental disorder, to choose certain values.

Berlin says that the man to whom it makes no difference whether he kicks a pebble or kills his family is mad, as a man who thinks he is Napoleon is mad. Well, this is compatible with Hume's position. For 1(a) (i.e., insanity) is compatible with Hume's position.

And, in a way it is a point in favour of this method that it can be used, without presupposing a particular view about the status of values, for if this method did presuppose a particular view about the status of values, then this method will appear suspicious to all those who do not share that view about the status of values.

I have in this section pointed out some difficulties involved in using this method, not in order to ridicule it, but for two reasons. Firstly, I tried to show that this method *can* be used by both objectivists and subjectivists, and that the subjectivists are not the only ones who will encounter difficulties in the use of this method. Secondly, I think this method should be used only in those cases where these difficulties have been overcome—I have not maintained that these difficulties are insurmountable, but only that they need to be surmounted if this method is to be used.

If this method is to be used to diagnose whether certain criminals are sick, then it would be a great help if those who are experts in this method could explain why certain criminal values are evidence of

madness, while certain other criminal values are not. Berlin says that certain scales of values are inhuman. But it is not enough to say that if a man has certain values then he remains human, but if he has certain others then he is inhuman. For what is meant by "human" and "inhuman"? If a man is inhuman can we infer that he is mad? It may be replied that if a dog or cat does not behave in a human way, this does not show that the dog or the cat is mad; but if a man behaves inhumanly this does show that he is disordered. Even if this reply is convincing, there is another problem still to be solved—viz., how do we decide which criminal values are inhuman and which criminal values are not inhuman?[16]

It may of course be that some people are good at getting the right answer to the question which values are inhuman, without being able to justify their answers. Just as *some* people are good judges of character, but if you ask them to justify their answers, they may not be able to do so.

But the trouble is that experts seem to disagree in their answer to the question which values are inhuman. Perhaps in some very extreme cases, there is more agreement, e.g., if someone really is indifferent between the destruction of his family and the kicking of a pebble, because both are antidotes to *ennui*, then there may be considerable agreement that this man is mad: but in less extreme cases there is likely to be considerable disagreement. Some capitalists may think that the values that Stalin pursued were inhuman, whereas the values that Hitler pursued were very wicked, but not inhuman. More left-wing people might say that the values that Hitler pursued were inhuman, that Hitler was a monster, while Stalin was very wicked, but not inhuman.

To some extent it may be inevitable that our own values should distort our judgments about human beings, but the less the distortion the better. That is why it would be a great help if people like Berlin

---

[16] The view that certain values are inhuman, while others are human, is I think *compatible* with the view that values do not exist in sense two. Thus a subjectivist could give as his reason for saying that certain values are human while others inhuman, that it is man who has created values and has loaded the term "human" with certain values, and the term "inhuman" with certain other values. It will then be an objective matter of fact that certain people, e.g., A, B, C, have values that are human, while certain other people, e.g., X, Y, Z, have values that are inhuman. But this objective fact is compatible with the subjectivist thesis that values do not exist in sense two.

The problem on this view would be with which values should we load the concept "human." And there may be considerable dispute on this problem between people who hold different moral views.

could also give us their justifications for saying that certain values are inhuman.

There is one important problem that needs to be discussed. What do we mean when we say that a man is "inhuman"? Is it just that he tends to choose *certain* ways of life? But then does not mental disorder connote passivity—the man suffering from mental disorder is not, or at least not fully, a choosing agent; he drifts, is passive, a victim of various forces, and not an active agent? And it may be objected, no amount of playing with words like "inhuman" can remove from us our burden of showing why a man, because he follows certain values, is not a choosing agent.

Our answer to this question could be that madness or mental disorder does not always connote that the person suffering from it is passive and drifting. This connotation is therewith an important sub-class of mad people (i.e., those suffering from cognitive or volitional disorder). But there is another class of mental disorder—consisting of people who have inhuman values, who are monsters, and not really human. These "monsters" know what they are doing, and also have control over their behaviour. They are choosing agents but are yet mad because they are monsters and not really human.

But then why should these monsters be excused from punishment? If they committed crimes, and if they were choosing agents, should they not be punished? It may be replied that if we do not have a common moral or social language with a criminal, then we should not punish him.[17] This does not of course mean that we should let such monsters loose on the community. We should lock them up but not punish them. Of course we need norms to tell us whether we have more of a common moral and social language with A than with B. For a lot will depend upon what respects are relevant and important.

Another way of tackling this problem would be to agree that mental disorder always implies that the capacity of choice is impaired, but that we need norms to decide which capacities really matter. For, at least in the cases of less severe abnormalities, those suffering from

---

[17] Gabriel de Tarde (*Freedom and Responsibility*, edited by H. Morris, pp. 46–49) believed that we excuse a man from punishment if he is not socially similar to us. And he tried to support this view by saying that this view explains why we excuse from punishment savages, epileptics, etc.

I think Tarde may be right that savages and epileptics are not socially similar to us, but I think these examples do not establish his case conclusively. For our reason for excusing savages and epileptics may be that such people have not had a fair opportunity of obeying our law.

such abnormalities lack a fair choice over a certain *important and worthwhile* range, but there will be other, less important and less worthwhile areas, where their power of choice may be unimpaired. Even psychotics and neurotics can do many things. And conversely, those we call sane cannot do many things. So we need norms to tell us which capacities are relevant for deciding whether a person is sane or mad.[18] But how is the use of norms in deciding whether someone is a choosing agent to be reconciled with the view that people are as a matter of objective fact either sane or not? I think the reconciliation comes about in this way: Given certain norms, it is a matter of objective fact that certain people are sane, while others are not.

I think now we may be able to see the sort of lines that those of us who want to excuse from punishment the psychopath, but not people like Russell and Gandhi, may be able to take. We could, with the help of norms, argue that we have a common moral and social language with Russell, but not with psychopaths. Or, alternatively, we could try to show with the help of norms that people like Russell are sane, while psychopaths are not. We could grant that the psychopath has certain capacities and lacks others. We could then argue that Russell too has certain capacities and lacks others. Thus, with regard to at least certain sensuous pleasures the psychopath may have capacities which people like Russell and Gandhi do not. But there are other capacities, e.g., the ability to make moral decisions, which people like Russell and Gandhi have, and which psychopaths lack—for psychopaths lack moral sentiments (even though they are capable of good theoretical reasoning in moral and intellectual matters). We could then use our norms to tell us that the capacities which psychopaths lack are relatively important, while the capacities that people like Russell lack are relatively unimportant. (And there is nothing odd in saying that the possession of some capacities is more important from the point of view of showing the man to be healthy, than the possession of others. Indeed, it would be odd if all capacities were treated as equally important.) So people like psychopaths are sick, while people like Russell are not. Now we saw in section one that a good case had been made for the view that, unlike some ordinary criminals, both psychopaths and people like Russell fail the second test. We have now seen the sort of lines along

---

[18] Earlier in this paper we say that the values that a man has may be used as evidence for mental disorder. Now we see that values enter in another way—we need them to tell us what the standards of mental disorder are.

Neither of these ways of bringing values into the problem of mental disorder presupposes that values exist in sense two.

which it could be argued that while psychopaths fail the second test because of sickness, people like Russell are not sick. In this way psychopaths, unlike people like Russell and Gandhi and unlike some ordinary criminals, could be excused from punishment.

APPENDIX

I have used two tests in deciding whether a man could have helped his criminal actions. I have appealed not just to how far a man could have acted otherwise at the time of committing the crime, but also to whether he could have done things in the past which would have prevented him from becoming a criminal later. Aristotle would have broadly agreed with this procedure. My main criticism of Aristotle was that he had wrongly applied these tests [e.g., he thought that all except the thoroughly senseless could have (in the past) helped acquiring wicked characters] *not* that he did not believe in these tests.

But Nowell-Smith has a more radical criticism against Aristotle's approach. He seems to think that Aristotle's appeal to what we could have done in the past is bound to lead us into inextricable difficulties. If Nowell-Smith is right, then I have been mistaken in appealing to how far we could have helped things in the past.

But I think Nowell-Smith's radical criticisms of the method of appealing to the past in order to decide issues of responsibility are not valid.

Nowell-Smith confuses the thesis of libertarians that to be free an action must be uncaused, with the thesis that we can often hold people responsible for getting into a muddle, even when once they have got into the muddle, they could not do much about it. (Even if Aristotle did believe in both these theses and confuse them with each other, yet it is valuable to distinguish them. Even if a search for uncaused actions does lead into inextricable difficulties, it is not obvious why we must cease to appeal to what we could have done in the past.) He then argues that a search for an uncaused action will lead us into inextricable difficulties. "You say that blaming me for doing x [now] is really blaming me for having done y and z [in the past]. Now apply the same argument to y and z and see where it leads you. Furthermore my ignorance at the time of doing y and z which, according to you, is the real source of the trouble, was not my fault either. My father did not have me properly educated. Blame him, if you must blame somebody; but he will offer the same reply as I have done, and so on ad infinitum . . . if we proceed on the assumption that, to be moral, an

action must be uncaused, either we shall find a genuinely uncaused action at the beginning or we shall not. If we do not, then, according to the libertarian, there can be no moral praise and blame at all (and it was to account for these that Libertarianism was invented); and if we do, we must suppose that, while almost all our actions are caused, and therefore amoral, there was in the distant past some one action that was not caused and for which we can be justly praised or blamed. This bizarre theory has in fact been held; but the objections to it are clear. We praise and blame people for what they do now, not for what they might have done as babies . . ."[19]

Now, of course, Nowell-Smith is quite right that we do not praise and blame men for what they might have done as babies; and if we were to adopt this strange practice, it would be most unjust. For people could not have helped what they might have done as babies. But why must an appeal to what we could have done in the past lead us into accepting this bizarre theory? To take into account how far one could have helped things in the past does not necessarily involve accepting the crude libertarianism that Nowell-Smith criticizes, *any more* than taking into account how far the criminal could have helped things at the time of committing the crime entails such libertarianism. If we allow that some actions can be helped at the time of committing the crime, then it seems odd to deny that some other actions, which could not be helped at the time of doing the act, could have been avoided in the past. What is absurd is the following thesis: we can *never* help things in the present, that all our present actions are the inevitable consequences of and constrained by our past actions, *and* that we are only responsible for what we did in the past. This thesis is absurd because the "past" too was at one time "present," and if all present actions are the inevitable consequences of and constrained by earlier ones, then to be consistent we must agree that the past actions too were just as much constrained as the present ones are.

But our thesis was not that no one can help things in the present, but that some people cannot, and of these some may still be held responsible if they could have helped things in the past. (Nor did Aristotle say that we can never help things in the present. It is true that he said about the unjust and the self-indulgent that once they have become so "it is not possible for them not to be so." But there are, according to Aristotle, other wrongdoers who can help things in the

present—some incontinent people would fall into this category. So Aristotle is not saying that blaming me for doing x [now] is *always* really blaming me for having done y and z [in the past].)

So to take into account how far things could have been helped in the past, does not involve the assertion that we can never help things in the present. We admit that sometimes people can help things at the time of committing the crime and this is relevant to issues of responsibility. The test that is concerned with how far we could have helped things in the past, does not replace the inquiry into how far we could help things in the present; it is an additional test that is to be used before we can say that a man could not have helped what he did. So by having this *additional* test, the result is that fewer people[20] would be excused than if we *only* inquired into how far the criminal could have helped things at the time of the crime. So Nowell-Smith is wrong in thinking that by appealing to how far people could have helped things in the past, we would be committed to excusing everyone. We certainly would not be committed to excusing more people than if we did not have this *additional* test.

[20] Though not as few as Aristotle thought. He wrongly thought that very few people (only the thoroughly senseless) would be excused.

ARISTOTLE'S DOCTRINE
OF JUSTICE*

Hans Kelsen

Thus the good, the moral value, is humanized; it is presented as virtue of man. Consequently the *Ethics* of Aristotle aims at a system of human virtues, among which justice is the "chief of the virtues," the "perfect virtue." How to determine the moral value, or, in Aristotle's language, the moral virtues? At the beginnings of his *Ethics*, Aristotle emphasizes that "the same exactness must not be expected in all departments of philosophy alike, any more than in all the products of arts and crafts." In the field of ethics "we must be content if, in dealing with subjects and starting from premises thus uncertain [as the concepts of the good and of justice], we succeed in presenting a rough outline of the truth . . ." "It is the mark of an educated mind to expect that amount of exactness in each kind which the nature of the particular subject admits. It is equally unreasonable to accept merely probable conclusions from a mathematician, and to demand strict demonstration from an orator." Nevertheless, Aristotle applies a mathematical-geometrical analogy to solve the central problem of his ethics, to answer the question as to what is virtue. It is his famous Doctrine of the Mean (*mesótes*). Virtue is a mean state between two extremes, which are vices, one of excess and one of deficiency. "Virtue is a mean state in the sense that it aims at hitting the mean . . . excess and deficiency are a mark of vice, and observance of the mean a mark of virtue."

This formula is—as Aristotle himself admits—instigated by a commonplace, "the common remark about a perfect work of art: that you could not take from it nor add to it;" which—according to Aristotle—means "that excess and deficiency destroy perfection, whereas adherence to the mean preserves it." Aristotle chooses this commonplace as starting point of his inquiry because in it the quality

* Reprinted from Hans Kelsen, *What Is Justice* (Berkeley and Los Angeles, 1960), pp. 117–136, by permission of the author and the University of California Press.

of value is presented as quantity; and the application of a mathematical-geometrical method in ethics is possible only if the moral value is transformed from a quality into a quantity. If the criterion of that which is good in a work is: that one cannot take away from it nor add to it, then the good is characterized in the same way as the point by which a line is divided into two equal parts. The moralist can find the virtue which he is looking for just as the geometrist can find the point equidistant from the two ends of a line. The tendency to quantify the moral value in order to render a mathematical-geometrical or quasi mathematical-geometrical method possible is very clear in the statement: "Now of everything that is continuous and divisible, it is possible to take the larger part or the smaller part, or an equal part, and these parts may be larger, smaller, and equal either with respect to the thing itself or relatively to us; the equal part being a mean between excess and deficiency. By the mean of the thing I denote a point equally distant from either extreme; which is one and the same for everybody; by the mean relative to us, that amount which is neither too much nor too little, and this is not one and the same for everybody." In another connection Aristotle says of the two vices between which, as between two extremes, the virtue as the mean lies: "The greatest degree of opposition exists between the two extremes. For the extremes are farther apart from each other than from the mean, just as great is farther from small and small from great than either from equal." That Aristotle intends to present his method of determining the moral good or virtue as a quasi mathematical-geometrical operation is shown by his saying that although it is possible to find what is good or a virtue, it is not easy: "It is a hard task to be good, for it is hard to find the middle point in anything: for instance, not everybody can find the center of a circle, but only someone who knows geometry." To determine the good is, in principle, the same problem as to determine the middle point of a straight line or the center of a circle.

The quantification of the moral value, the three-partite scheme of "too much," "mean," "too little," the essential presupposition of a mathematical-geometrical method of determining the good, is a fallacy. In the realm of moral values there are no measurable quantities as in the realm of reality as object of natural science. Ethics deals with qualities only—with the qualities of good and evil, right and wrong, just or unjust, virtuous or vicious; that is to say, with conformity and nonconformity to a norm presupposed as valid. The statement that a definite human behavior is good or evil, right or wrong, just or unjust, virtuous or vicious, presupposes the assumption that something ought

to be done. The statement that something ought to be, or to be done, is a norm. It is a way to express the idea that something is an end, not a means to an end. It is a value judgment. The statement that a human behavior is good or evil, right or wrong, just or unjust, virtuous or vicious, means that this behavior is in conformity with a presupposed norm, or is not in conformity with it, that is, in contradiction to the presupposed norm. If a man's behavior is in conformity with a norm presupposed to be valid, we say: he obeys the norm; if his behavior is not in conformity with the norm, because it contradicts the norm, we say: he violates the norm.

The statement that a virtue is the mean between a vice of deficiency and a vice of excess, as between something that is too little and something that is too much, implies the idea that the relationship between virtue and vice is a relationship of degrees. But, since virtue consists in conformity, and vice in nonconformity of a behavior to a moral norm, the relationship between virtue and vice cannot be that of different degrees. For with respect to this conformity or nonconformity no degrees are possible. A behavior can neither "too much" nor "too little" conform, it can only conform or not conform to a (moral or legal) norm; it can only contradict or not contradict a norm. If we presuppose the norm: men shall not lie, or—expressed positively —men shall tell the truth, a definite statement made by a man is true or is not true, is a lie or is not a lie. If it is true, the man's behavior is in conformity with the norm; if it is a lie, the man's behavior is in contradiction to the norm. But the behavior cannot be in different degrees in conformity with or in contradiction to the norm. It cannot be more or less and, hence, not too much or too little in conformity or contradiction to the norm. Aristotle's differentiation of three degrees or "amounts"—excess, mean, deficiency—does, in truth, not refer to the moral value, the quality of being good or evil, a virtue or a vice, but to a psychic reality. He says: Moral virtue "is concerned with feelings and actions, in which one can have excess or deficiency or a due mean. For example one can be frightened or bold, feel desire or anger or pity, and experience pleasure and pain in general, either too much or too little, and in both cases wrongly; whereas to feel these feelings at the right time, on the right occasion, toward the right people, for the right purpose, in the right manner, is to feel the best amount of them which is the mean amount—and the best amount is, of course, the mark of virtue." Applied to the virtues of temperance and courage, the *mesótes* doctrine is presented as follows: "The observance of the mean of fear and confidence is courage. The man that exceeds in fearlessness is not

designated by any special name (and this is the case with many of the virtues and vices); he that exceeds in confidence is Rash; he that exceeds in fear and is deficient in confidence is Cowardly. In respect of pleasures and pains—not all of them, and to a less degree in respect of pains—the observance of the mean is Temperance, the excess Profligacy. Men deficient in the enjoyment of pleasures scarcely occur, and hence this character also has not been assigned a name, but we may call it Insensible." Cowardice is a "vice of deficiency," because it is characterized by too little confidence. Rashness is a "vice of excess," because it is characterized by too much confidence. Profligacy is a vice of excess, because it is characterized as too much indulgence in pleasure. Insensibleness is a vice of deficiency, because it is characterized by too little enjoyment of pleasure. The feeling which accompanies or causes a certain behavior may be capable of different degrees of intensity but not the conformity or nonconformity of this behavior with the moral norm which constitutes the virtue or the vice, the quality of being right or wrong. Neither of these degrees or amounts is, in itself, "too much" or "too little," or represents excess or deficiency. To be "too much" or "too little," are value judgments which are possible only if one presupposes that a certain degree or "amount" is the "right" one. And a certain degree or amount of feeling is "right" because the behavior accompanied or caused by this feeling is right, that is, in conformity with the moral norm. What is right or wrong is the behavior in its relation to the moral norm; and this relation is not capable of degrees. This is why Aristotle cannot consistently maintain his statement that the virtue is a mean, and, as such, opposed to the extremes, but has to admit that virtue is an extreme itself. He is compelled to modify his doctrine of the mean by saying that virtue is "the observance of the mean" only "in respect of its essence and the definition that states its original being," but "in point of excellence and rightness it is an extreme." The point of excellence and rightness is in truth the only point which counts, for virtue is by its very nature "excellence and rightness." The ideas of "too much" and "too little," designating a quantitative distance from the good, are merely figures of speech, a special metaphor in presenting the relation of a human behavior to a moral (or legal) norm. Aristotle compares the fact that a certain behavior corresponds to a presupposed norm with the middle point of a line, and the fact that a behavior does not correspond to a presupposed norm with the two ends of the line. When the phenomenon is described without using a metaphor, the tripartite scheme of the *mesótes* formula must immediately be replaced by a bipartite scheme:

the antagonism of good and evil, right and wrong, conformity and nonconformity. "Too much" and "too little" are not—as the doctrine of the mean presents them—two different quantities of the same moral substratum, but two different expressions designating one and the same quality, namely nonconformity—the fact that a certain behavior contradicts a norm. Virtue means: to comply with a moral norm, vice: to violate a moral norm.

To distinguish between two different vices as two different "extremes" is possible only if there are two different norms regulating human behavior. It seems that this is the situation at least in some cases to which the *mesótes* formula is applied. A typical example is the virtue of courage as a mean between the vice of cowardice as "too little" and the vice of rashness as "too much" (confidence). By characterizing the vice of cowardice as compared with the virtue of courage as "too little" we express figuratively the idea that the behavior in question contradicts the norm whose fulfillment constitutes the virtue that the coward violates, the norm prescribing courage. By characterizing the vice of rashness compared with the virtue of courage as "too much" we express the idea that the behavior contradicts a norm other than the one whose fulfillment constitutes the virtue concerned. Only rashness, the "too much," not cowardice, the "too little," is a violation of the norm prescribing courage. A rash man is courageous, whereas a coward is not. The former is courageous but he has too much confidence. In this sense he is "too" courageous; and that means that he, by being courageous, violates another norm, the one prescribing prudence, the duty to take into consideration the possibility of success, the principle that the value we risk to destroy should be in a certain proportion to the value we try to realize by our action. "Too" just is, according to a widespread opinion, he who applies a certain rule of international morality in a certain case even to the disadvantage of his own country, who in applying this rule violates the norm expressed in the well-known saying: "right or wrong, my country." In one of the two "too's" of the *mesótes* formula nonconformity to one norm, in the other nonconformity to another norm is expressed. In the spatial metaphor that virtue is the mean between two vices as two extremes, one conformity is brought in relation to two nonconformities, without expressing the fact that there are two different norms which the two patterns of behavior, characterized as "vices," are violating. The *mesótes* doctrine creates the appearance as if it were one and the same norm which one violates by, so to speak, remaining below, or by going beyond the line determined by it. The

mesótes formula veils the problem it pretends to solve. Since the norms of a given moral system are very often in conflict with one another, it is necessary, in order to act morally, to restrict the sphere of validity of the different norms in the proper way. That "virtue" is the "mean" between two vices means that morally correct is only the behavior by which the one of the conflicting norms is obeyed without the other being violated. The true problem is to show how this is possible, how, for example, a man's behavior can conform to the norm of courage and at the same time to that of prudence. To this question the *mesótes* doctrine gives no answer; nor to any question aiming at a determination of the moral value.

It claims to be such an answer by pretending to furnish a method by which the moralist can find the good by finding the mid point between two vices, just as geometry furnishes a method to find the middle point between two extreme points of a line. If the *mesótes* formula is a determination of the good at all, it is it only if the virtue is a mean in the same sense as a line is bisected at a point equidistant from its two ends. But this Aristotle cannot maintain. For the two vices between which the virtue lies are not extremes in the same sense as the two ends of a line bisected at a point equidistant from them. This is shown by an example Aristotle himself presents. He says: "Suppose that ten pounds of food is too much for anybody and two pounds too little, it does not follow that a trainer will prescribe six pounds [which is the exact mean], for perhaps even this will be too much or too little for the particular athlete who is to receive it." If the "extremes"—ten and two—can be characterized only as "too much" and as "too little," any quantity greater than ten—that is, the one characterized as "too much"—is also too much, and any quantity smaller than two—that is, the one characterized as "too little"—is also too little, and the correct quantity may be any of the infinitely many magnitudes between ten and two. This is the reason why Aristotle distinguishes between the mean in an objective sense and the mean in a subjective sense of the term, between the "mean with respect to the thing" which is the real mean, and "one and the same for everybody," and the "mean with respect to us," which "is not one and the same for everybody." That expresses that the "mean with respect to us" is not determined and not determinable as the point equidistant from the two ends of the bisected line. Virtue is a mean between two vices in the sense of the "mean with respect to us." Since the two "extremes" between which virtue lies as a "mean with respect to us" are not so determined as the two extreme points of a line must be determined in order that we can determine the

point equidistant from them—since the two vices are characterized only as "too much" and "too little"—all we can say of the virtue we are looking for is that it lies somewhere between them. There is no reason to assume that the virtue lies exactly in the middle and not nearer to the one or the other vice. Aristotle admits: "In some cases the defect, in others the excess, is more opposed to the mean; for example, Cowardice, which is a vice of deficiency, is more opposed to Courage than is Rashness, which is a vice of excess; but Profligacy, or excess of feeling, is more opposed to Temperance than is Insensibility, or lack of feeling." Later he says: "This much then is clear, that it is the middle disposition in each department of conduct that is to be praised, but that one should lean sometimes to the side of excess and sometimes to that of deficiency, since this is the easiest way of hitting the mean and the right course." If one leans to the side of excess or to the side of deficiency, one does not hit the mean, but one may hit the right course. Hence, virtue is not the "mean" but the "right course." One of the definitions of virtue runs as follows: "Virtue, then, is a settled disposition of the mind as regards the choice of actions and feelings, consisting essentially in the observance of the mean relative to us, this being determined by a rational principle, that is, as a man of practical wisdom would determine it."/According to the original formula of the *mesótes* doctrine, the mean is determined by the two extremes. But the "mean relative to us" is not determined in this way and hence no "mean" at all. It is determined by "practical wisdom," and "practical wisdom issues commands, since its end is what ought to be done or not to be done"—it coincides in Aristotle's ethics with the moral order. Hence virtue is that disposition of men that is in conformity with the moral order. This is the true meaning of the statement that virtue is the observance of the mean relative to us./

The statement that a virtue lies somewhere between two vices is a figure of speech. Its meaning, without the use of a metaphor, is: if we compare a virtue with two vices, the virtue is neither the one nor the other vice. The *mesótes* formula amounts to the tautology that: if something is correct it is not too much and not too little—or, in other words, that a virtue is not a vice, that good is not evil, right is not wrong.

But even if the two moral extremes were as completely determined as the two extreme points of a line bisected at a point equidistant from the two ends, and even if the moral mean were not a "mean with respect to us, but a mean with respect to the thing," and consequently as determined and determinable as the point equidistant

from the two ends of the bisected line, the *mesótes* formula were no determination of the moral good. The alleged determination of the good consists in the statement that the virtue is a mean between two opposite vices. The existence of these vices Aristotle takes for granted. He does not prove that the two extremes, as for instance rashness and cowardice, are evils or vices; his ethics presupposes it as self-evident; just as a geometrist presupposes a circle or the two extreme points of a line as given in order to determine the center or the point by which the line is divided into two equal parts. The circle or the two extreme points being given, that is, predetermined, the determination of the center or the bisecting point is automatically implied. The center is determined by the given circle, the middle point of a line by the two given extreme points.

If an ethical doctrine presupposes all possible vices, it presupposes, together with those vices, all possible virtues. If we know what is evil, we thereby know what is good, and then nothing new remains to be determined. Even if the virtue determined according to the *mesótes* formula as a mean between two "given" vices, were "a mean with respect to the thing" and hence "one and the same for everybody," the formula could proclaim only a redundancy. For its meaning were, in this case too, nothing else but that the good is opposite to the evil; and the evil is not determined but presupposed by the formula.

Although the ethics of the *mesótes* doctrine pretends to establish in an authoritative way the moral value, it leaves the solution of its very problem to another authority: the determination of what is evil or a vice, and, consequently, also the determination of what is good or a virtue. It is the authority of the positive morality and the positive law—it is the established social order. By presupposing in its *mesótes* formula the established social order, the ethics of Aristotle justifies the positive morality and the positive law which, as a matter of fact, determine what is "too much" and what "too little," what are the extremes of evil or wrong, and thereby what is the mean, that is, good and right. In this justification of the established social order lies the true function of the tautology which a critical analysis of the *mesótes* formula reveals.

The book v of Aristotle's *Ethics*, devoted to the problem of justice, begins with the question: "In regard to justice and injustice (*dikaiosýne* and *adikía*) we have to inquire what sort of actions precisely they are concerned with, in what sense justice is the observance of a mean, and what are the extremes between which that which

is just is a mean. Our inquiry may follow the same procedure as our
preceding investigations." It is the procedure of the *mesótes* doctrine.
Aristotle first distinguishes justice in a general and justice in a particular sense. There are, he maintains, two concepts of justice: lawfulness
and equality. "The term 'unjust' is held to apply both to the man who
breaks the law and the man who takes more than his due, the unfair
man. Hence it is clear that the law-abiding man and the fair man will
both be just. 'The just' therefore means that which is lawful and that
which is equal or fair, and 'the unjust' means that which is illegal and
that which is unequal or unfair." As to the relationship between
lawfulness and equality, Aristotle says that the two concepts are not
identical, lawfulness being the broader, equality the narrower concept:
Not everything unlawful is unequal, though everything unfair is
unlawful. Equality is related to lawfulness "as part to whole." Consequently justice in the sense of lawfulness is "not a part of virtue but
the whole of virtue"; it is perfect virtue "with a qualification, namely
that it is displayed toward others." That means that justice in the sense
of lawfulness is a social virtue. By lawfulness Aristotle undoubtedly
understands conformity to positive law. He says: "We saw that the
lawbreaker is unjust and the law-abiding man just. It is therefore clear
that all lawful things are just in one sense of the word, for what is
lawful is decided by legislature, and the several decisions of legislature
we call rules of justice." The *nómimon* is identical with the *díkaion,*
law identical with justice (in one sense of this term). But is *nómos,* the
law, really to be understood as the positive law—any positive law?
This question must certainly be answered in the affirmative. For
Aristotle continues: "Now all the various pronouncements of the law
aim either at the common interest of all, or at the interest of a ruling
class determined either by excellence or in some other similar way; so
that in one of its senses the term just is applied to anything that
produces and preserves the happiness, or the component parts of the
happiness, of the political community." But the "happiness" may be
the happiness "of all" or only of "a ruling class." It is this justice in the
general sense of lawfulness which Aristotle characterizes as the "perfect virtue" and the "chief of virtues, and more sublime than the
evening or the morning star." Which amounts to an unconditional
glorification of positive law. But Aristotle is not a positivist. He does
not confine his inquiry to an analysis of positive law, he does not
renounce the use of the two concepts of justice and law, the *díkaion*
and the *nómimon;* he maintains the dualism, but only to identify
positive law with justice, to justify the *nómimon* as *díkaion.*

/Of the particular justice, which consists in equality, there are also two kinds: distributive and corrective justice. Distributive justice "is exercised in the distribution of honor, wealth, and the other divisible assets of the community which may be allotted among its members in equal or unequal shares" by the legislator. Corrective justice is "that which supplies a corrective principle in private transactions . . . those which are voluntary and those which are involuntary." The corrective justice is exercised by the judge in settling disputes and inflicting punishments upon delinquents. The principle of distributive justice is proportional equality. That "justice involves at least four terms, namely two persons for whom it is just and two shares which are just. And there will be the same equality between the shares as between the persons, since the ratio between the shares will be equal to the ratio between the persons: for if the persons are not equal, they will not have equal shares." Thus the principle of distributive justice is expressed in a mathematical formula: If a right a is allotted to an individual A, and a right b to the individual B, the requirement of distributive justice is fulfilled if the ratio of value a to value b is equal to the ratio of value A to value B. If the individuals A and B are equal, the rights to be allotted to them must be equal too. However, there are in nature no two individuals who are really equal, since there is always a difference as to age, sex, race, health, wealth, and so forth. There is no equality in nature. Nor is there equality in society./Equality as a social category, the statement that two individuals are socially equal, does not mean that there are no differences between these individuals, but that certain differences which really exist, as for instance differences concerning age, sex, race, wealth, are considered to be irrelevant. The decisive question as to social equality is: Which differences are irrelevant?/To this question Aristotle's mathematical formula of distributive justice has no answer. Nor to the other essential question as to which rights the legislator ought to allot to the individuals in order to be just. Is it just to confer upon the citizens the right of private property, or is it just to establish communism? Is it just to confer upon the citizens political rights, that is, to establish democracy, or is it just to confer upon the citizens no political rights at all, to establish autocracy? /Aristotle's formula of distributive justice says only, that *if* rights are allotted, and *if* two individuals are equal, equal rights shall be allotted to them. According to this formula a capitalistic as well as a communistic legal order is just, and a legal order which confers political rights only to men who have a certain income, or who belong to a certain race, or are of noble birth is as just as a legal order which confers the

same rights to all human beings who are of a certain age without regard to other differences. Any privilege whatever is covered by this formula. When a legal order reserves all possible rights to one single individual (the ruler) and assigns only duties to all others (the ruled), such a legal order too is just, since the difference between the ruler and the ruled is considered to be decisive, so that the ruled cannot be considered as equal to the ruler.

To illustrate his formula of distributive justice Aristotle refers to the "principle of assignment by desert." He says: "All are agreed that justice in distributions must be based on desert of some sort, although they do not all mean the same sort of desert; democrats make the criterion free birth; those of oligarchical sympathies, wealth or, in other cases, birth; upholders of aristocracy make it virtue." But his moral philosophy is not capable and considers itself not competent to answer the question which of these criteria is the just one. This, however, is the very question of justice.

The answer to this question Aristotle's *Ethics* leaves to the authority of positive law. Only if it is supposed that the positive law decides the question which rights shall be conferred upon citizens, and which differences between them are relevant, Aristotle's mathematical formula of distributive justice is applicable. As a postulate it means nothing else but that positive law shall be applied according to its own meaning. The equality of this justice is the equality before the law, which means merely legality, lawfulness. Aristotle's definition of distributive justice is but a mathematical formulation of the well-known principle *suum cuique*, to each his own, or to each his due. But this tautology has the important function of legitimizing the positive law which, as a matter of fact, fulfills the task, which legal philosophy is not capable of fulfilling—to determine what is everybody's due.

"Corrective" justice is exercised by the judge in deciding cases of "voluntary or involuntary transactions." "To go to a judge is to go to justice, for the ideal judge is, so to speak, justice personified." Aristotle's distinction between "voluntary" and "involuntary" transactions probably coincides by and large with our distinction between civil and criminal law. He says: "Examples of voluntary transactions are selling, buying, lending at interest, pledging, lending without interest, depositing, letting for hire; these transactions being termed voluntary because they are voluntarily entered upon. Of involuntary transactions some are furtive, for instance, theft, adultery, poisoning, procuring, enticement of slaves, assassination, false witness. Others are violent, for instance, assault, imprisonment, murder, robbery with violence, maim-

ing, abusive language, contumelious treatment." All these acts are crimes which are punishable under positive law. Corrective justice, too, is equality; but it is equality not according to geometrical but according to arithmetical proportion; it is not equality of two ratios, it is equality of two things, especially of two losses or two gains. A typical example is barter, which may stand for any voluntary trans-action. Corrective justice requires that the service and counterservice constituting the barter should be equal. The loss of one party by doing a service to the other party ("doing a service" comprising also making a gift to the other party) shall be equal to the loss of the latter by doing a return service ("doing a return service" comprising also giving a return gift); and vice versa: the gain of one party in receiving service from the other should be equal to the gain of the latter by receiving a return service from the former. The same equality shall prevail in the relation between crime and punishment. To do a service to another without receiving from him an adequate return service amounts to the same injustice as to commit a crime without receiving the adequate punishment. The problem of this kind of justice is: what is the adequate, correct, just return service, the adequate, correct, just punishment? Aristotle tries to answer this question, too, by a mathe-matical-geometrical formula. He compares the situation when a man has done to another a service without receiving a return service, or when a man has committed a crime injuring another, with a line divided into unequal parts. "The unjust being here the unequal, the judge endeavors to equalize [the inequality] . . . the judge endeavors to make them [the two parts of the line] equal by the penalty or loss he imposes, taking away the gain." "Now the judge restores equality: if we represent the matter by a line divided into two unequal parts, he takes away from the greater segment that portion by which it exceeds one-half of the whole line, and adds it to the lesser segment. When the whole has been divided into two halves, people then say that they 'have their own,' having got what is equal. . . . The equal is a mean by way of arithmetical proportion between the greater and the less. For when of two equals a part is taken from one and added to the other, the latter will exceed the former by twice that part, since if it had been taken from the one but not added to the other, the latter would exceed the former by once the part in question only. Therefore the latter will exceed the mean by once the part, and the mean will exceed the former, from which the part was taken, by once that part." The two equal parts of a bisected line and the two halves of a whole are evidently only a metaphor for the relationship of equality which

should be established between service and return service, crime and punishment. The metaphor is no solution of the problem of just return service and just punishment. It is only another way of presenting the problem. Aristotle, however, thinks that by stating that the judge has to find the mean in the same way a geometrist divides a given line into two equal parts, he has solved the problem of corrective justice. He says with reference to the just quoted passage: "This process then will enable us to ascertain what we ought to take away from the party that has too much and what to add to the one that has too little." That means: the process enables us to determine the just return service and the just punishment; "we must add to the one that has too little the amount whereby the mean between them exceeds him, and take away from the greatest of the three the amount by which the mean is exceeded by him." All this says nothing else but that service and return service, that crime and punishment should be equal. This equality is certainly not a mathematical quantitative equality. An exchange between two persons takes place if both need different things. Aristotle says: "An association for interchange of services is not formed between the physicians, but between a physician and a farmer, and generally between persons who are different [i.e., who are able to do different services] and who may be unequal [with respect to their services] though in that case they have to be equalized." That means: service and return service have to be equalized, since they are in themselves not and cannot be, equal in the sense the two halves of a line are, nor can crime and punishment be equal in this sense.

This is why Aristotle is compelled finally to give up his mathematical formula according to which "equality" is established by corrective justice. In discussing the Pythagorean doctrine that justice is reciprocity (*antipeponthós*) he says that reciprocity is sometimes at variance with corrective justice. But he admits: "In the interchange of services justice, in the form of reciprocity, is the bond that maintains the association; reciprocity, that is, on the basis of proportion, not on the basis of equality. The very existence of the state depends on proportionate reciprocity, because men demand that they shall be able to requite evil with evil (if they cannot, they feel they are in the position of slaves) and to repay good with good (failing which, no exchange takes place, and it is exchange that binds them together)." The principle of retribution, or—more, generally formulated, reciprocity—is the rule to return evil for evil, good for good, like for like. The punishment shall be equal to the crime, the reward equal to the merit. The decisive question, what is evil and what is good, is not

answered by this formula; nor the question, what is "like" or equal. Positive law is, by its very nature, a coercive order. It provides coercive acts—forcible deprivation of life, freedom or property—as sanctions to be executed against the individual who commits a delict, that is, behaves in a way considered by the legislator to be harmful to society. The different legal orders differ very much in their determination of the delicts as well as the sanctions; but all correspond to the principle of retribution, which is at the basis of the social technique we call law. That retribution is considered as a principle of justice may be explained by the fact that it originates in one of the most primitive instincts of man, his desire for revenge. Aristotle's objection against the rule "like for like" as principle of justice, is that the relation between merit and reward, crime and punishment is not equality but proportionality. Return service shall not be equal to the service, the punishment not equal to the crime—this is impossible—but "proportional," which means that the one should be in an adequate proportion to the other. But this again is merely a presentation, not the solution, of the problem. The decisive question as to what is corrective justice remains unanswered. The pretended answer is a mere sham answer. It is again the tautology of the formula, "To each his own."

Although the discussion of the problem of justice starts with the question in what sense justice is the observance of a mean, the *mesótes* doctrine plays but a subordinate role in Aristotle's legal philosophy. The application of the *mesótes* formula to the problem of justice is superficial and not very consistent. The sense of the statement that justice is a mean is not always the same. The main statement is: "Just conduct is a mean between doing and suffering injustice, for the former is to have too much and the latter to have too little." It is evident that one of the two extremes (doing injustice and suffering injustice), namely, suffering injustice, is no vice. The *mesótes* formula has here a meaning different from that which it has in the discussion of the other virtues. This is admitted by Aristotle himself. He says: "Justice is a mode of observing the mean, though not in the same way as the other virtues are." The difference is of no interest here, since the *mesótes* formula in its application to the problem of justice has the same character of a tautology as in its application to the other moral values. This character is here even more obvious. Doing injustice and suffering injustice are not two different degrees of one and the same substratum; they are not even two different facts between which a third fact can be situated. One man's doing injustice implies another man's suffering injustice. The one cannot be separated from the other.

To say that justice is a mean between doing and suffering injustice, is a figurative expression of the judgment that justice is not injustice, neither the injustice which is done, nor the injustice which is suffered, which, however, are both one and the same injustice.

It might seem as if Aristotle himself was not completely satisfied with the result of his doctrine of justice. For in book viii of his *Ethics*, where he discusses the virtue of friendship, a certain tendency appears to complete the more or less empty idea of justice by the more substantial idea of peace. Here we read the astonishing passage: "Friendship appears to be the bond of the state; and lawgivers seem to set more store by it than they do by justice; for to promote concord, which seems akin to friendship, is their chief aim; while faction [discord], which is enmity, is what they are most anxious to banish. And if men are friends there is no need of justice between them; whereas merely to be just is not enough; a feeling of friendship also is necessary." "Concord" means peace; and to establish peace rather than justice seems to be—according to this statement—the essence of the state. Aristotle does not disapprove that legislators aim chiefly at peace, not at justice; and where peace prevails there is no need of justice. Justice is not enough! Is that the same justice of which Aristotle so enthusiastically speaks at the beginning of his inquiry into the nature of this virtue, proclaiming it "the chief of virtue," and "more sublime than the evening or the morning star"? Since to establish peace is certainly a function of the law, the stress Aristotle lays on the idea of peace corresponds to his identification of justice with law. "Justice," says Aristotle in his *Politics*, "is a function of the state. For the law is the order of the political community; and the law determines what is just." If it is the law which determines what is just, justice is lawfulness; and if justice is equality, it is only equality before the law.

This definition of justice as equality before the law implies the substitution of the logical value of truth for the moral value of justice.

Since a rationalistic moral philosophy is not capable of determining the content of a just order, of answering the questions what is good and what is evil, which differences between individuals are relevant and which irrelevant, who is equal and what is equal, it must presuppose these determinations. This means: leave it to the state (that is, to the positive legislator) who establishes a legal order, a system of general norms to be applied by the judge. When the legislator has established an order, when, for example, he has stipulated that every male citizen more than 24 years old may participate in the election of the magistrates, or that every individual more than 14 years old who

commits theft shall be punished, and so on, then moral philosophy is in a situation to ascertain that it is just to allow not only A but also B to exercise a right of voting, provided that both are equal, that is, male citizens, 24 years of age; and that it is just for the judge to punish not only C but also D, provided that both individuals are equal, namely, both are more than 14 years old and both have committed theft. This is the principle of justice in the sense of lawfulness or in the sense of equality; this is equality before the law. And this kind of equality is established by any general norm. Equality before the law is maintained when the general norm is applied according to its own meaning. This is why this kind of equality is identical with lawfulness. If the judgment is valid that every individual more than 14 years old who has committed theft shall be punished, and if C and D are both individuals more than 14 years old who have committed theft, then the judgment is true that not only C but also D shall be punished. It is true as a conclusion from the general to the particular, which is implied in the application by a judge of a general norm to a particular case. If a judge, pretending to apply a general rule of law, states that C shall be punished and D shall not be punished, he presupposes in the first case the general judgment: Every individual more than 14 years old who has committed theft shall be punished; and in the second case, the general judgment: Not every individual more than 14 years old who committed theft shall be punished. These two general judgments constitute a logical contradiction. The judgment that it is not just to decide that C shall be punished but D shall not be punished, only means: it is contradictory. The principle of justice in the sense of equality before the law or lawfulness is nothing but the logical law of contradiction with reference to the application of a general norm of positive law to particular cases. This is the only concept of justice which Aristotle's moral philosophy—as any other rational philosophy —is able to define.

It is obvious that this concept of justice, as a law of thought, is totally different from the original ideal of action we understand by justice. This ideal does not aim at a logically, but a morally satisfactory normative system. A totally noncontradictory order as a system of general rules may be totally unjust in the original sense of the ideal. The substitution of the logical value of noncontradiction for the moral value of justice, inherent in the definition of justice as equality before the law, is the result of the attempt to rationalize the idea of justice as the idea of an objective value. Although this substitution is no solution, but an elimination of the problem of justice, it seems that the attempt

will never be abandoned—perhaps, because of its important political implication. This type of rationalistic philosophy, pretending to answer the question what is just, and hence claiming authority to prescribe to the established power how to legislate, ultimately legitimizes the established power by defining justice as equality before the law and thus declaring the positive law to be just.

Since the concept of justice produced by a rationalistic moral philosophy has no definite content, it must not necessarily be used in a conservative tendency, to legitimize the given social order, to justify the validity of positive law. It may be used—although the intellectual history of mankind shows that this is only exceptionally the case—in a reformatory, or even revolutionary, tendency, to deny the validity of a given social order by declaring it unjust. A very interesting example is the legal philosophy of Aurelius Augustinus, who was a bishop of the Christian Church in an African province of the Roman Empire at a time when this empire was not yet a firmly established province of Christianity. Augustine identifies law and justice, just as Aristotle identifies the *nómimon* and the *díkaion;* but he does so, not as Aristotle did, in order to strengthen the authority of the former by that of the latter. He propounds the thesis that a social order is law only if it is just, in order to destroy the authority of Roman law. "Where there is no true justice" he says, "there can be no law. For what is done by law is justly done, and what is unjustly done cannot be done by law. For the unjust inventions of men are neither to be considered nor spoken of as laws; for even they themselves say that law is that which flows from the fountain of justice, and deny the definition which is commonly given by those who misconceive the matter, that right is that which is useful to the stronger party. Thus, where there is not true justice there can be no assemblage of men associated by a common acknowledgement of law," that is, a state. "If there is no law where there is no justice then most certainly it follows that there is no state where there is no justice." "Justice taken away, then, what are states but great robberies?"

But what is justice? To this question Augustine answers with the same formula which Aristotle used to an exactly opposite purpose. "Justice is that virtue which gives everyone his due." But what is everyone's due? The Greek philosopher left the answer to the authority of the positive moral and legal order accepted by the majority of his society, the Christian bishop to the positive religious order of the minority to which he belonged. According to Augustine, justice is Christianity, injustice paganism. "Where, then, is the justice of man,

when he deserts the true God and yields himself to impure demons? Is this to give every one his due? Or is he who keeps back a piece of ground from the purchaser, and gives it to a man who has no right to it, unjust, while he who keeps back himself from the God who made him, and serves wicked spirits, is just? . . . Hence, when a man does not serve God, what justice can we ascribe to him? . . . And if there is no justice in such an individual, certainly there can be none in a community composed of such persons." Consequently—and the Saint does not hesitate a moment to face this consequence—there never was a Roman State. Which amounts to saying: there never was a Roman law.

This is a very interesting result of a doctrine of justice based on the empty tautology of the formula "To every one his due." It is interesting not so much because this formula enables the one who is willing to use it, to deny to an empire (by which, during many hundred years, a great and the most civilized part of mankind, was organized) the character of a state, and to a law (which was so to speak the mother of all modern law) the character of law; it is so interesting because it shows the unlimited possibility of using this formula to any purpose whatever.

SUGGESTED FURTHER READINGS

TRANSLATIONS OF THE NICOMACHEAN ETHICS

One should always remember that Aristotle wrote in Greek, and so too much weight should not be placed on the wording of any single translation. Something one sees in one translation but not in others is quite possibly not in the original, either. We recommend two translations: one by Martin Ostwald (New York: Bobbs-Merrill, Library of Liberal Arts, 1962); the other by W. D. Ross (London: Oxford University Press, The Student's Oxford Aristotle, 1942). The Ostwald translation is more readable and provides useful notes and a glossary of important terminology. Ross is more literal, occasionally perhaps gaining in accuracy at the expense of ready intelligibility; he provides a useful index.

INTRODUCTIONS TO ARISTOTLE'S PHILOSOPHY

Allan, D. J. *The Philosophy of Aristotle*. London: Oxford University Press, 1952.

Randall, J. H., Jr. *Aristotle*. New York: Columbia University Press, 1960.

Ross, W. D. *Aristotle*. New York: Meridian Books, Inc., 1959.

STUDIES OF ARISTOTLE'S ETHICS AND RELATED TOPICS

Allan, D. J. "Individual and State in the *Ethics* and *Politics*," in *La Politique d'Aristote*. Geneva: Fondation Hardt, Entretiens, 1964, XI, 55–85.

Ando, T. *Aristotle's Theory of Practical Cognition*. Kyoto: T. Ando, 1958.

Burnet, J. *The Ethics of Aristotle*. London: Methuen and Co., 1900. This is a Greek text, but the introduction and extensive notes are unusually interesting.

Gauthier, R.-A. *La morale d'Aristote*. Paris: Presses Universtaires de France, 1958.

———, et J. Y. Jolif. *L'Ethique à Nicomaque*, 3 vols. Louvain: Publications universitaires de Louvain, 1958, 1959. This is the most valuable single reference work, containing a lengthy introduction, a French translation arranged according to speculations about the original editing, and a monumental bibliography.

Jaeger, W. "Aristotle's Use of Medicine as a Model of Method in his Ethics," *Journal of Hellenic Studies*, LXXVIII (1957), 54–61. Reprinted in his *Scripta Minora*. Roma: Edizioni de Storia e Letteratura, 1960, II, 491–509.

Joachim, H. H. *Aristotle, The Nicomachean Ethics, A Commentary*, ed. D. A. Rees. Oxford: The Clarendon Press, 1951.

Stewart, J. A. *Notes on the Nicomachean Ethics of Aristotle*, 2 vols. Oxford: The Clarendon Press, 1892.

Walsh, J. *Aristotle's Conception of Moral Weakness*. New York: Columbia University Press, 1963.

STUDIES OF SPECIAL RELEVANCE TO SELECTIONS
IN THIS VOLUME

Gauthier

Prichard, H. A. "Does Moral Philosophy Rest on a Mistake?" *Mind*, XXI (1912). Reprinted many times—for instance, in H. A. Prichard, *Moral Obligation*. Oxford: The Clarendon Press, 1949, pp. 1–17.

Siegler

Hardie, W. F. R. "The Final Good in Aristotle's Ethics," *Philosophy*, XL (1965), 277–295.

Dewey

Kolnai, A. "Deliberation Is of Ends," *Proceedings of the Aristotelian Society*, 1961–1962, pp. 195–218.

Anscombe

Allan, D. J. "The Practical Syllogism," in *Autour d'Aristote*. Louvain: Publications universitaires de Louvain, 1955, pp. 325–340.

Anscombe, G. E. M. *Intention*. Oxford: Basil Blackwell, 1957.

Jarvis, J. "Practical Reasoning," *The Philosophical Quarterly*, XII (1962), 316–328.

Mothersill, M. "Anscombe's Account of the Practical Syllogism," *Philosophical Review*, LXXI (1962), 448–461.

Santas, G. "The Socratic Paradoxes," *Philosophical Review*, LXXIII (1964), 147–164. Reprinted in A. Sesonske and N. Fleming, eds., *Plato's Meno: Text and Criticism*. Belmont, Calif.: Wadsworth Publishing Company, 1965, pp. 49–64.

Ryle

Allan, D. J. "Aristotle's Account of the Origin of Moral Principles," *Actes du XIe Congrès international de philosophie*. Amsterdam: North-Holland Publishing Company, 1953, XII, 120–127.

Haksar

Aristotle, *Eudemian Ethics*, trans. H. Rackham. London: William Heinemann Ltd., "The Loeb Classical Library," 1952. The discussion of voluntariness and the various moral dispositions is somewhat fuller and slightly different from that found in the *Nicomachean Ethics*.

Hart, H. L. A. "The Ascription of Responsibility and Rights," in *Logic and Language*, first series, A. G. N. Flew, ed. Oxford: Basil Blackwell, 1952, pp. 145–166.

Kelsen

Feinberg, J. "Justice and Personal Desert," in *Justice*, C. Friedrich and J. Chapman, eds. New York: Atherton Press, 1963, pp. 69–97.
Ladd, J. "The Place of Practical Reason in Judicial Decision," in *Rational Decision*, C. Friedrich, ed. New York: Atherton Press, 1964, pp. 126–144.